Promoting
Belonging, Growth Mindset,
and **Resilience** to Foster Student Success

Amy Baldwin, Bryce Bunting, Doug Daugherty, Latoya Lewis, and Tim Steenbergh

Cite as:
Baldwin, A., Bunting, B., Daugherty, D., Lewis, L., & Steenbergh, T. (2020). *Promoting belonging, growth mindset, and resilience to foster student success.* Columbia, SC: University of South Carolina, National Resource Center for The First-Year Experience & Students in Transition.

ISBN: 978-1-942072-37-9
Published by:
National Resource Center for The First-Year Experience® and Students in Transition
University of South Carolina
1728 College Street, Columbia, SC 29208
www.sc.edu/fye

The First-Year Experience® is a service mark of the University of South Carolina. A license may be granted upon written request to use the term "The First-Year Experience." This license is not transferable without written approval of the University of South Carolina.

Production Staff for the National Resource Center:

Project Manager:	Tracy L. Skipper, Assistant Director for Publications
Design and Production:	Stephanie L. McFerrin, Graphic Artist
External Reviewers:	Peter Arthur, University of British Columbia
	Lisa Marie Kerr, University of Alabama at Birmingham

Library of Congress Cataloging-in-Publication Data

Names: Baldwin, Amy, 1973- author. | Bunting, Bryce D., 1981- author. | Daugherty, Doug, author. | Lewis, Latoya, 1978- author. | Steenbergh, Timothy A., author.
Title: Promoting Belonging, Growth Mindset, and Resilience to Foster Student Success / Amy Baldwin, Bryce Bunting, Doug Daugherty, Latoya Lewis, and Tim Steenbergh.
Description: Columbia, SC : National Resource Center for The First-Year Experience and Students in Transition, University of South Carolina, 2020. | Summary: "This book aims to deepen the conversation about the noncognitive factors that significantly impact student success. Not just a book about how to support the development of learning mindsets such as belonging, growth mindset, and resilience in students, it will also include strategies for college personnel to consider as they create initiatives, programs, and assessments to develop these noncognitive factors"-- Provided by publisher.
Identifiers: LCCN 2019005234 (print) | LCCN 2019022037 (ebook) | ISBN 9781942072379 (pbk.) | 9781942072386
Subjects: LCSH: Learning, Psychology of. | Belonging (Social psychology) | Academic achievement. | Resilience (Personality trait)
Classification: LCC LB1060 .B3535 2020 (print) | LCC LB1060 (ebook) | DDC 370.15/23--dc23
LC record available at https://lccn.loc.gov/2019005234
LC ebook record available at https://lccn.loc.gov/2019022037

Contents

Tables and Figures

Tables

Figures

Foreword

Greg Walton, Associate Professor of Psychology
Stanford University

Everyone who has gone to college can tell their own story of belonging. What do we do when we go to college? We leave home communities and families to travel, sometimes across the country and sometimes across town, to join a new community. We meet new peers and hope they will become our friends but fear we might be excluded. We interact with instructors in new ways and hope they will value and respect us and help us grow but fear they might judge us lacking. We get lost on a vast new campus and hope we can find our way. College comes with all the predictable worries and fears of a major life transition.

For me, the transition was represented most memorably by, of all things, a food truck. You see, I came to college in California from the Midwest, and somehow, I'd gotten it into my head to worry what California would be like and whether I might belong among Californians. I had every advantage coming to college. My parents both have graduate degrees; in fact, both are professors. And I am White, so no one was going to judge me as lacking on the basis of my social class or race/ethnicity.

But this wasn't just any food truck. It was an In-N-Out Burger truck, from a franchise of overwhelming popularity in California but unknown in the Midwest, and it showed up on campus one day my first autumn in college. All my new classmates, my ostensible friends-to-be, lined up to get In-N-Out burgers while I marched off in a disgruntled mess to the dining hall, thinking, "I'm not going to stand in line for an hour for a burger." For my classmates, In-N-Out represented home. For me, it meant difference.

All students traverse a social distance in coming to college. For many thousands of students, this distance is far greater than what I traveled. Students who are the first in their family to come to college may wonder if they will belong among peers with different backgrounds, who may hold different values; they may worry about losing family and friends back home. Black, Latinx, and Native American students might wonder if people will view them as tokens of a stereotyped group rather than as individuals who are, like others, struggling to learn and find their footing as young adults. Women in math, science, and engineering may worry that they will be excluded from male peer groups or unable to access equal opportunities to learn. Faced with a history of disadvantage and current inequalities, it's easy to wonder, "Does someone like me belong in college?"

As a social psychologist working with colleges and universities for the past 15 years, I have had the opportunity to learn about the experiences of students and reflect on the ways we can improve higher education. This work has been guided by the belief that students' perspectives matter. In one of my first studies, Geoff Cohen and I gave Black and White college students a seemingly simple task. We asked students to list their friends who would fit in well in the field of computer science. Some students were asked to list two friends—that was easy, and both Black and White students were reasonably optimistic about their belonging and potential to succeed in the field. Other students were asked to list eight friends—that was hard for all participants. The question was, What inference, if any, would students draw because they had difficulty listing eight friends? The answer was that White students remained sanguine, but Black students assessed their prospects far worse. In fact, whereas Black students in the list-two-friends condition rated their potential to succeed in computer science at the 58th percentile (i.e., slightly above average, among classmates), those asked to list eight friends rated their potential at just the 31st percentile. And they thought more about race and began to discourage another Black peer from pursuing the field. It was as if the difficulty they experienced listing eight friends meant that they might not belong in the field—and that their group might not either.

From an outsider's point of view, difficulty listing friends might seem like a small thing. But in many ways, it is reasonable for students to enter college with persistent worries about belonging—and from that perspective, even everyday challenges can speak to these core concerns. Black students, for instance, enter college aware of the underrepresentation of their group in higher education, of opposition to its inclusion, and of longstanding racial stereotypes that demean their intelligence and work ethic. Fears about belonging are magnified when a campus police officer interrupts a Black graduate student taking a nap in a common area by saying, "We need to make sure that you belong here," as happened at Yale in the spring of 2018. Given this sociocultural context, it is easy to wonder whether one will truly be valued and respected, especially in the core academic spaces of college. Within that context, everyday experiences like a brusque exchange with a professor or exclusion from a peer study group can readily take on larger meanings.

That's why it's so important to think carefully about how we welcome students to college. And it's important—but not enough—to consider the "objective" experiences students have. We must also consider how we lead students to make sense of their experiences, especially challenges they face. Can we create experiences, communicate messages, and build a campus culture that helps students understand common worries and challenges as normal obstacles that can be overcome?

Targeted messages can be effective. In one study, Geoff Cohen and I brought Black and White first-year college students into a laboratory and shared stories about the transition to college from a diverse group of more advanced students. The stories all conveyed a basic truth: Nearly everyone worries at first about whether they belong in college, but it gets better with time. The idea was to get students out of a fixed mindset about belonging—a way of thinking in which people analyze daily events to determine whether they mean "I belong" or "I don't belong." Instead, we wanted students to see belonging as a process that grows and develops with time, one they could promote (to ask: "How can I build my belonging here?"). We asked students to reflect on the stories and write their own stories about how they too had worried about belonging when coming to college and how this concern had changed with time. Students were told their stories could be shared with future students to help them in their transition to college, but the most important purpose was to help students think deeply about their experience of belonging through the structure provided by the older students' stories.

This hour-long experience, which we call the social-belonging intervention, proved transformational for Black students. As compared to a randomized control condition, Black students who completed the treatment exercise earned higher grades over the rest of their college careers, cutting by half the racial achievement gap from sophomore through senior year. And they reported being happier and healthier at the end of college. How did the intervention produce these benefits? First, it shifted how students made sense of their stream of daily experience. These students did not interpret daily challenges like feelings of homesickness or academic criticism as meaning that they did not belong in college. Second, by sustaining this sense of belonging, the intervention helped Black students stay engaged and reach out more on campus—studying more, emailing professors more, and building more friendships and mentor relationships. When students saw challenges to belonging as normal and as improving, they built more of the resources that all students need to succeed in college.

Later studies suggested that this basic approach can be effective with other populations as well, including women in male-dominated engineering fields and students who face racial and socioeconomic disadvantages in college, including Black, Latinx, and first-generation college students. Moreover, versions of the intervention can be placed online to reach tens of thousands of students, improving academic and social outcomes. Thanks to the work of the College Transition Collaborative, we are rapidly learning more about for whom and in what contexts the intervention is more and less effective.

The research shows what is possible, but brief, standalone interventions can only go so far. What happens during the other 99.99% of a college student's experiences? How can we create cultures on campus that support belonging and growth? That's where *Promoting Belonging, Growth Mindset, and Resilience to Foster Student Success* comes in.

Welcome! You have before you an extraordinary set of wisdom. Leading scholars and educators Amy Baldwin, Bryce Bunting, Doug Daugherty, Latoya Lewis, and Tim Steenbergh showcase effective ideas and tools from the worlds of both research and practice. Every chapter includes a learning mindset story—so we can hear people's experiences in their own words and understand how they have made sense of challenges they have faced.

Each chapter also includes tips for starting campus conversations and next steps so you can begin a dialogue on your own campus to create positive change.

There are important lessons here for researchers, too. Continuing the long tradition of research inspired by the wisdom of practice, the authors suggest numerous opportunities for researchers to learn from promising practices and to examine and isolate those practices to understand their impact for students and college communities.

Every year, approximately 17 million people enroll in undergraduate degree programs in the United States. Welcome to a journey—one we take together in many roles, to learn more about students' experiences and to make actual environments of belonging and growth for the diverse population of students we serve.

Preface

Bryce Bunting

During the 18 months we worked together to move our thinking about growth mindset, belonging, and resilience from presentation slides to a formal proposal to this completed book, we frequently found ourselves sharing our own stories related to the themes we were writing about. Some stories were from our work as learners and teachers, whereas others were of growth and resilience from students we have come to know. Rarely did our team of five coauthors come together and not engage in some sort of storytelling.

Over time, these stories became powerful anchors for our writing. This book has been influenced by the formal, theoretical, and research-based story of learning mindsets, and it has also been shaped by our lived experiences as learners, teachers, partners, and parents engaged in pursuing our own growth and supporting others in theirs. Telling, retelling, and hearing these secret stories of struggling through challenges, working to belong, and responding with resilience (Clandinin & Connelly, 1996) have been just as important in guiding our thinking and writing.

Similarly, we recognize that you, as readers, bring your own stories of growth, belonging, and resilience to the book. Just as our stories have become intertwined with the broader metastory we have provided, we hope that yours will provide an equally important lens through which to engage with, critique, and make meaning of the research and strategies we share in what follows.

It is common for readers to wonder: Why this book? And why now? These are fair and important questions that we frequently reflected on while writing. It is customary for scholarly works to address such questions, and we do that in the Introduction. We provide a scholarly explanation for the book following the unstated rules for developing research questions and book ideas. The standard (and rather romanticized) script for developing a book dictates that, among other things, it should be grounded in theory, respond to glaring gaps in the literature, and be born out of stimulating dialogue that seems to take place over drinks, with colleagues, at academic conferences, in exciting cities.

To be fair, our book does follow that script, and we have worked to ground it in good theory. We hope to help bridge a gap between theory and practice, and we first began to discuss the idea of the volume while together at a conference sponsored by the National Resource Center for The First-Year Experience and Students in Transition (to whom we owe a tremendous debt of gratitude for supporting our writing).

To encourage engagement in this reflective process, we have included a Learning Mindset story for each chapter, highlighting the experiences of students, faculty, and staff members and the ways that their beliefs about learning and development shaped their experiences. These stories play a pivotal role in the book. Our aim is to introduce and illustrate key concepts, add a human element to each chapter, and help readers begin to consider where they might have encountered similar situations in their own work.

As readers engage with these stories, as well as with the research and recommendations that follow, we hope they will begin reflecting on, telling, and retelling their own learning mindset stories. In fact, one measure of the success or impact of this book will be the degree to which it becomes a catalyst for crafting, sharing, and refining new narratives, grounded in theory and informed by local knowledge. We also invite readers to consider stories that come to mind from an institutional point of view as they read the book and (ideally) discuss it with colleagues. To help initiate such storytelling, we have included "Campus Conversations" prompts and practical "Next Steps" for supporting student success. These institutional stories and reimaginings of the student experience will provide powerful vision and commitment for the work ahead.

We conclude this preface with one of our own personal learning mindset stories. Other stories are drawn from our personal experiences and those of students with whom we have worked. Ultimately, we hope these stories, combined with the concepts introduced throughout the book, illustrate the powerful impact that students' views toward learning and school (i.e., their mindsets) can have on nearly every aspect of their college experience.

Bryce's Mindset Story: Reflecting Across the Academic Lifespan

When I was young, my teachers told me I was smart and that I would become someone important, like a doctor. I was frequently praised for my grades, and I learned to play the game of school by putting in as little effort as possible for the maximum reward. Outside of math, which I believed I had a knack for, I avoided most academic challenges and enrolled in classes I knew wouldn't stretch me too much. Case in point: The schedule for my senior year of high school included study hall, an athletic training internship that on most days involved taping a few ankles and then relaxing in the training room for the rest of the hour, and "home release." No, I was not incarcerated. But I somehow managed to obtain formal permission to spend the first class period of each day at home ... sleeping.

My only real academic challenge that year was AP Calculus. In that class, I worked very hard because I believed I could pass the AP exam. That perspective did not extend to other subjects, however. I was particularly terrified of the arts and writing, convinced that I had not been gifted any artistic genes and that no amount of work or effort would translate into success in those subjects. I took this perspective into my first year of college and declared athletic training as my major. It was familiar, and I felt like I belonged in that world, both because I was an athlete and because I had a good foundation in the sciences.

For reasons I no longer remember, and despite my aversion to the subject, I enrolled in a first-year honors writing course. The first major assignment was a three-page essay analyzing a work of poetry from our textbook. Naturally, I chose the shortest poem, which proved problematic because it left me with very little grist for the analytic mill. After a sleepless night looking at a blank computer screen, I managed to write (almost) three pages and finished the essay a few hours before my 8 a.m. class.

I knew my analysis was weak, but I hoped my mediocre effort would be enough for the same high grades I had grown accustomed to in high school. It wasn't. I earned a C+, by far the lowest grade in my academic career to that point. This experience reinforced my belief that I was not a writer and didn't belong in any academic program that required writing or creative work.

Looking Inward

Two years later, I transferred to a new school and changed my major to physical education because, again, it was familiar and allowed me to (mostly) avoid writing and the arts. Around the same time, I was hired as a peer mentor in my school's first-year experience (FYE) program. At that point, some subtle but important changes began to happen.

The director of the program (who was also a psychologist) told me about an interesting book called *Mindset* (Dweck, 2006) and recommended that I take a look. As I read, she also suggested that I do some reflective writing about my reaction to Dweck's ideas and how they connected with my own experiences.

For the next few months, I met with the director weekly to add to my reading list; to discuss ideas such as mindset, grit, and resilience, which were new to me; and to think about what those might mean for the FYE at our institution. It did not take long to recognize that, for most of my school career, I had firmly believed my academic success came from innate intelligence or talent (Dweck, 2006). Even more painful was the guilt I felt about preaching a *growth mindset* to the first-year students I had been assigned as a peer mentor. This gap between how I had operated as a student to that point and what I was expected to model and convey to new students was critical in helping me adopt a new mindset. It also contributed greatly to the way I saw myself as a learner in a university context.

Ultimately, those last few years of my undergraduate experience were transformative. Over time, as I learned alongside faculty mentors and others, I began to feel that I had found my place on campus. My perspective toward learning shifted, I started to embrace challenges and believe I could be successful if I worked hard, and I felt safe involving others in my learning. Remnants of my previous mindset occasionally surfaced—I still sometimes chose easy classes, and I put the thought of graduate school out of my mind because it seemed like too much of a stretch. But I was changing in important ways.

The Power and Potential of Mindsets

These sorts of developmental journeys toward productive mindsets have the potential to change students' academic trajectories. Distilled to their core, the underlying message of most learning mindset stories, including Bryce's, is that as students reframe their views toward learning and school, their behaviors change and they position themselves to take greater advantage of the opportunities for learning and growth inherent in their college environment.

Reflecting on our own experiences with learning mindsets and engaging with the stories of others has taught us that nearly every learning mindset story includes a common set of key factors. We invite readers to pay attention to those factors. For example:

- What types of relationships support learning mindsets?

- What role does reflection play?

- What types of experiences might inadvertently reinforce unproductive or fixed mindsets? and, most important,

- What elements of experience support students in adopting a growth mindset, feeling a sense of belonging on campus, and responding to adversity with resilience?

By reflecting on and formulating answers to such questions, you will better understand the research associated with learning mindsets and be well positioned to design experiences—both in and out of the classroom—that foster student success.

References

Clandinin, D. J., & Connelly, F. M. (1996). Teachers' professional knowledge landscapes: Teacher stories—stories of teachers—school stories—stories of schools. *Educational Researcher, 25*(3), 24-30.

Dweck, C. S. (2006). *Mindset: The new psychology of success.* New York, NY: Random House.

Introduction

Defining Student Success

Bryce Bunting

Although traditional measures of academic performance—GPA, test scores, and graduation rates, to name a few—will likely always be used to define college student success (at least in part), a more holistic definition has emerged over the past two decades (Astin, 1993; Felten, Gardner, Schroeder, Lambert, & Barefoot, 2016; Kuh, Kinzie, Schuh, & Whitt, 2005; Light, 2001; Schreiner, Louis, & Nelson, 2012). This broadened view of success includes the development of traditional academic skills (Association of American Colleges & Universities [AAC&U], 2002, 2005), encompassing discipline-specific skills, critical-thinking abilities, competence in written and oral communication, and the ability to solve complex problems. It also considers social and emotional well-being (Schreiner et al., 2012), with increased emphasis on supporting students in establishing meaningful relationships (e.g., Chambliss & Takacs, 2014; Mayhew et al., 2016; Upcraft, Gardner, & Barefoot, 2005) and developing the ability to work collaboratively with others (e.g., AAC&U, 2005). Finally, post-graduation outcomes such as employability, civic engagement, and overall life satisfaction are increasingly considered key indicators of student success (e.g., Kuh, Kinzie, Buckley, Bridges, & Hayek, 2007; Perna & Thomas, 2008).

It is worth noting that all these ways of defining student success are largely administrative or institutional measures. Indeed, common metrics such as student retention, educational attainment, academic achievement, and student advancement are terms we are much more likely to hear in meetings of institutional leaders than in conversations with students. Of course, students care about test scores, developing academic skills, graduating, and finding employment. However, they also measure their success based on the extent that they feel that they belong and have meaningful and supportive relationships, and on whether the time and effort invested in their learning makes a real difference in their performance (Asher & Weeks, 2014; Cook-Sather, 2018; Strayhorn, 2012).

For the purposes of this book, we have chosen to define student success in very holistic terms, in alignment with our view that, ultimately, institutions of higher education are responsible for supporting students' development as whole people. A survey of institutional mission statements and goals—nearly all of which outline objectives that extend beyond narrow definitions of academic achievement—would also support this definition. This is not to say measures such as retention, persistence, and graduation rates should be of no concern. Rather, experiences at our own institutions, as well as mounting evidence from higher education research, strongly point to the need to view student success from a much broader perspective.

In short, when we refer to student success throughout the remainder of the book, we are referring to an expanded definition: a holistic phenomenon that includes intellectual, emotional, social, ethical, physical, and spiritual development (Cook-Sather, 2018; Cuseo, 2007). Ultimately, we assert that the primary purpose of higher education is to support students in becoming learners (Sanders, 2018) and that success is really about the degree to which students experience learning, growth, improvement, and change (Dweck, 2006) across a variety of domains—both in and outside the classroom.

Although it is clear that a complex interplay of personal and environmental factors influences this type of holistic success, getting one's head around the idea can be challenging. We find Astin's (1991) I-E-O model very helpful in that respect. The model recognizes that college student inputs (e.g., demographics, background, prior experiences) interact with the college environment (e.g., programs, policies, relationships, experiences on campus) to influence student outcomes. From this perspective, success is determined both by students' personal characteristics and by the nature of their experiences once they arrive on campus (e.g., courses taken, interactions with faculty, peer associations, cocurricular involvement, residential life).

Building on this work, Kuh and others argued that the single best predictor of college success is the time and energy students invest in *educationally purposeful activities* (Kuh et al., 2005). The authors drew increased attention to the critical role institutions play in (a) organizing and providing access to these high-impact activities and (b) encouraging students to become involved in them.

In sum, the past two decades of research on the college experience support two important conclusions. First, what students do really matters. Second, what institutions do is just as important. This includes not only the types of experiences provided to students but the ways that institutions—both explicitly and implicitly—encourage investment of time and energy in these educational offerings. Thus, college success is a shared responsibility between students and the institution, particularly those at the institution who interact with students in an educational capacity (e.g., faculty, academic advisors, staff).

The Promise of Research for Narrowing the Achievement Gap

Although what students *do* is a key factor in their academic performance, it is increasingly clear that student success also depends greatly on what students *believe*, both about themselves as learners and about their learning environment. Psychological research has provided valuable insight into the ways students' internal beliefs, attitudes, and self-perceptions influence their engagement and success (Farrington et al., 2012). Indeed, recent research examining various psychosocial interventions demonstrates that targeting students' beliefs about learning (e.g., the nature of intelligence, their sense of belonging, their interpretation of failure) helps to shift their behaviors and engagement so that they benefit more fully from the programs, experiences, and resources at higher education institutions. In short, by focusing on what students believe, we affect what they do and how they engage with the educational environment.

This approach holds particular promise with regard to the nearly ubiquitous focus among policy makers, higher education leaders, and government officials on increased success as measured by college enrollment and graduation rates. Typically, these efforts are based on the evidence that college success yields benefits for graduates personally and for communities that reap the rewards of educated citizens (Lobo & Burke-Smalley, 2018).

Consequently, stakeholders from across higher education have worked to address important issues of access, equity, and achievement. And although these efforts have yielded some gains—enrollment in college has increased dramatically in recent years, for example—new challenges have emerged. For instance, persistence has declined significantly during the same period (Baum, Ma, & Payea, 2013; Ost, Pan, & Webber, 2018). The reality is that we face an urgent need to better understand and address the factors that promote college success, both in traditional ways (i.e., retention, persistence, and graduation) and measures of personal learning, growth, and holistic development.

Research on learning mindsets holds tremendous promise for these efforts, particularly as it relates to closing the achievement gap[1]. As explained more fully in the chapters that follow, positive learning mindsets are important for all college students but are particularly critical for underrepresented minorities, those of lower socioeconomic status, and others from disadvantaged backgrounds (Sisk, Burgoyne, Sun, Butler, & MacNamara, 2018; Walton & Cohen, 2011; Yeager et al., 2016). In fact, learning-mindset interventions are shown to have an outsized impact on these segments of the college student population. These interventions are associated with reduced levels of stereotype threat (Steele, 2010), higher levels of engagement in positive academic behaviors, and increased resilience in the face of academic and social challenges (Farrington et al., 2012). This book makes an important contribution to the dialogue around closing the achievement gap and contains helpful tools for institutional leaders, classroom instructors, academic advisors, and others who work to foster success among all students on campus.

A Note on Terminology: What Do We Call This Stuff?

Although there is general consensus that a broad range of behaviors, attitudes, and strategies heavily influence student success, there is far less agreement over what to call this

---

[1] An achievement gap is present "when one group of students [such as students grouped by race/ethnicity, gender] outperforms another group and the difference in average scores for the two groups is statistically significant [that is, larger than the margin of error]" (NCES, 2018).

constellation of key factors. Common umbrella terms include *21st century skills, character strengths, social skills,* and *soft skills.*

Twenty-first century skills is a fairly broad term frequently used in business and technology circles referring to life and career skills; information, media, and technology skills; and learning skills (e.g., critical thinking, communication, collaboration, and creativity; Partnership for 21st Century Learning, 2015). *Character strengths* grew out of the character education movement in the United States and came into vogue in the 1980s and 1990s (Peterson & Seligman, 2004). One example is New York City's KIPP public charter schools and their character curriculum, which includes grit, zest, optimism, self-control, gratitude, social intelligence, and curiosity (KIPP Public Charter Schools, 2018). *Social skills* include interpersonal abilities such as cooperation, assertion, responsibility, and empathy (Farrington et al., 2012). Finally, employers commonly refer to *soft skills* as nearly any attribute or quality that allows one to interact effectively with others or as part of a group.

Another common descriptor for these attributes is *noncognitive factors.* This broader term refers to a more expansive collection of skills, strategies, attitudes, and behaviors that positively influence academic performance but are not measured by traditional cognitive or standardized tests (Farrington et al., 2012; see also Heckman, 2008; Nagaoka et al., 2013; Sparkman, Maulding, & Roberts, 2012). Although strong evidence suggests that these factors affect student performance, the term *noncognitive* is problematic, as it suggests that (a) students' beliefs about learning are not related to cognitive processes or (b) certain learning strategies and behaviors take place in the absence of cognition (Borghans, Duckworth, Heckman, & ter Weel, 2008; Bransford, Brown, & Cocking, 2000; Farrington et al., 2012). Despite such criticism, the term has become embedded in the dialogue among educational leaders, policymakers, researchers, and even practitioners. To synthesize the research literature in this area, Farrington et al. (2012) outlined a conceptual framework comprising five broad categories: academic behaviors, academic perseverance, academic mindsets, learning strategies, and social skills.

This book focuses on a subset of these factors, namely growth mindset (Dweck, 2006), belonging, and resilience. We collectively refer to these factors as *learning mindsets* to reflect that the remainder of the book focuses specifically on how students' beliefs, attitudes, and ways of thinking shape behavior and performance. We also want to emphasize the impact these mindsets have not only on traditional measures of academic performance but on learning more broadly. As learning mindsets are key determinants in what students actually learn, our goal is to persuade readers that these mindsets have broad application across learning contexts, both in and outside of formal academic environments.

Why This Book? Why Now?

In recent years, research on the influence of learning mindsets on student success has proliferated. Best-selling books, including *Mindset* (Dweck, 2006), *Grit* (Duckworth, 2016), and *Whistling Vivaldi* (Steele, 2010), have focused attention to this area of research. TED Talk videos, articles in mainstream magazines, and a cottage industry of guidebooks and resources for teachers, coaches, parents, and others have grown more common. Although early work on mindsets may have focused on K-12 settings, this research is increasingly recognized for its potential to influence higher education.

Much scholarly literature has also been published on the subject, providing critical theoretical understanding of the psychological processes that affect student learning as well as strong empirical evidence of the efficacy of various psychological interventions. As a result, student affairs professionals and institutional leaders continually look for practical strategies and interventions that have a positive impact on students' growth mindset, sense of belonging, and capacity for resilience. This hunger for practical guidance is evident in the proliferation of conference presentations, workshops, and other how-to resources aimed at supporting students in developing productive learning mindsets. However, these efforts to develop and implement mindset-focused programming and interventions must be grounded in sound psychological principles to be effective.

In writing this book, we saw a need to bridge the gap between the scholarly literature on academic mindsets and the opportunities and challenges specific to higher education practice. Our book responds to this need by providing a concise review of relevant literature with an eye toward higher education contexts. Along the way, we offer concrete and practical strategies for fostering student success through programming, intentional experiences, and interventions demonstrated to positively shape students' learning mindsets.

For Whom Was This Book Written?

Supporting student success is not about a single person, program, or policy. Rather, it hinges on institutions' ability to create campuswide communities and cultures that include well-articulated and agreed-upon priorities, an openness to innovation and change, and a coordinated approach to infusing mindset messaging and practices across the undergraduate experience. Consequently, this book is for anyone with a stake in this work, including:

- student affairs practitioners charged with developing, implementing, and refining student success programming and interventions;
- faculty members and others who engage with students in the classroom; and
- institutional leaders responsible for providing vision and shaping their school's culture around student success.

Again, we have written to a broad and somewhat varied audience to reflect the reality that this work requires campuswide efforts. Every member of an institution's campus community plays an important role in influencing students' sense of belonging, mindset toward learning, and resilience in the face of challenges.

Structure and Organization

In keeping with the overarching goal of providing practical, research-based recommendations for strengthening students' learning mindsets, we have organized the book around a core set of questions:

- What are the key learning mindsets?
- When, where, and how can we most effectively support students in developing productive learning mindsets?
- How can institutions create an institution-wide culture of growth, belonging, and resilience?
- How can institutions assess and evaluate their efforts to strengthen students' learning mindsets?

These questions provided general guidance as we conceptualized the book, and in some cases we opted to devote entire chapters to addressing them.

In Chapter 1, we provide an overview of the research on noncognitive factors, including definitions and descriptions of key constructs. We also discuss the rationale for giving particular attention to growth mindset, belonging, and resilience.

In Chapter 2, we discuss the importance of learning mindsets during times of transition, the role of these mindsets in the first-year experience, and research-based recommendations for developing effective mindset interventions for first-year students. In Chapter 3, we highlight the applicability of learning mindset research in the classroom, provide examples of effective strategies for supporting productive learning mindsets, and discuss how classroom practices can contribute more broadly to institutional culture.

We turn our attention to the achievement gap and reexamine the research on learning mindsets in Chapter 4, with an eye toward developing strategies and interventions that offer particular promise for supporting students from underrepresented minority groups. We devote Chapter 5 to exploring the relationship between campus culture and students' learning mindsets.

The role of learning mindsets in professional development—for faculty, staff, and peer leaders—is the focus of Chapter 6. In Chapter 7, we introduce the concept of growth-oriented assessment and give examples of strategies for assessing mindset-focused interventions and programming. In the Appendix, we also offer a glossary of terms that appear throughout the volume.

In addition to research-rich content and relevant practical strategies, each chapter includes a set of common features:

- **Learning Mindset Story:** Each chapter opens with a narrative or vignette highlighting a student, faculty member, or staff member and describing how their mindset, resilience, or belonging shaped their experiences. These stories provide helpful context for each chapter and are designed to spark reflections on readers' own learning mindset stories. Throughout the book, we have changed names and identifying information to protect individuals' privacy.

- **Campus Conversations:** We hope readers will invite others—including faculty, staff, student leaders, administrators, and community partners—to read and discuss this book. To facilitate such dialogue, we conclude each chapter with a set of questions for promoting reflection, discourse, evaluation of existing practices, and a vision for the future.

- **Next Steps:** In combination with the "Campus Conversations" feature of each chapter, this section supports readers in outlining action steps and implementing meaningful change as it relates to learning mindsets.

An Invitation to Readers

An inherent danger in writing a theory-to-practice book like this one is that some readers may be seeking a one-size-fits-all strategy, intervention, or program that will improve students' mindsets and foster success in an almost magical way (see Yeager & Walton, 2011 for a more in-depth discussion of this tendency as it relates to social–psychological interventions). However, in sharing concrete strategies and examples of successful interventions, we do not mean to suggest these are appropriate for all students or for every institution. Providing such a magic bullet was never our intent, and readers searching for one will be disappointed.

What we hope to illustrate is that the most successful interventions include essential psychological (and theory-based) components that lead to positive changes in students' thoughts and feelings about learning. Additionally, effective interventions are always context-specific, meaning they must be adapted to fit the unique aspects of the context in which they are implemented.

Consequently, we invite readers to identify the theoretical bases of each intervention shared, look for common elements or principles of the effective practices described, and then reflect on and discuss with colleagues how to apply or implement these elements in their own contexts. Supporting students' learning and growth requires an integrated, holistic, and campuswide approach that engages all stakeholders. These efforts should be responsive to institutional history, local challenges and opportunities, and the unique needs of students at a particular college.

Fostering student success through the development of productive mindsets and feelings of belonging involves much more than developing a single premier program or high-impact intervention. Rather, the greater task is for institutional teams to bring together a constellation of effective, research-based practices that, together, create a culture of growth, belonging, and resilience. This type of culture is most likely to emerge when students, faculty, and staff strive together to do the collective work of learning and share responsibility for ensuring that all members of the community feel like they belong.

Accordingly, while we hope this book leads to the development of new programs, interventions, and the like, our more proximal goal is that it serve as a catalyst for dialogue and debate around the ideas we present; clarified vision among campus leaders for how learning mindsets might be cultivated at their institutions more fully; new research on the role of learning mindsets in college student success; and, perhaps most important, renewed confidence and inspiration for the critical, daily work of supporting students in their learning.

References

Asher, S. R., & Weeks, M. S. (2014). Loneliness and belongingness in the college years. In R. J. Coplan & J. C. Bowker (Eds.), *The handbook of solitude: Psychological perspectives on social isolation, social withdrawal, and being alone* (pp. 283-301). New York, NY: John Wiley & Sons.

Association of American Colleges & Universities. (2002). *Greater expectations: A new vision for learning as a nation goes to college.* Washington, DC: Author.

Association of American Colleges & Universities. (2005). *Liberal education outcomes: A preliminary report on student in achievement in college.* Washington, DC: Author.

Astin, A. W. (1991). *Assessment for excellence: The philosophy and practice of assessment and evaluation in higher education.* Washington, DC: American Council on Education/Oryx Press Series on Higher Education.

Astin, A. W. (1993). *What matters in college? Four critical years revisited.* San Francisco, CA: Jossey-Bass.

Baum, S., Ma, J., & Payea, K. (2013). *Education pays 2013: The benefits of higher education for individuals and society.* New York, NY: The College Board.

Borghans, L., Duckworth, A. L., Heckman, J. J., & ter Weel, B. (2008). The economics and psychology of personality traits. *Journal of Human Resources, 43*(4), 972-1059.

Bransford, J. D., Brown, A. L., & Cocking, R. R. (2000). *How people learn: Brain, mind, experience, and school.* Washington, DC: National Academy Press.

Chambliss, D. F., & Takacs, C. G. (2014). *How college works.* Cambridge, MA: Harvard University Press.

Cook-Sather, A. (2018). Listening to equity-seeking perspectives: How students' experiences of pedagogical partnership can inform wider discussions of student success. *Higher Education Research & Development, 37*(5), 923-936.

Cuseo, J. (2007). Defining student success: The critical first step in promoting it. *E-Source for College Transitions, 4*(5), 2-5.

Duckworth, A. (2016). *Grit: The power of passion and perseverance.* New York, NY: Scribner.

Dweck, C. S. (2006). *Mindset: The new psychology of success.* New York, NY: Random House.

Farrington, C., Roderick, M., Allensworth, E., Nagaoka, J., Keyes, T., Johnson, D., & Beechum, N. (2012). *Teaching adolescents to become learners. The role of noncognitive factors in shaping school performance: A critical literature review.* Chicago, IL: University of Chicago Consortium on Chicago School Research.

Felten, P., Gardner, J. G., Schroeder, C. S., Lambert, L. O., & Barefoot, B. O. (2016). *The undergraduate experience: Focusing institutions on what matters most.* San Francisco, CA: Jossey-Bass.

Heckman, J. J. (2008). Schools, skills, and synapses. *Economic Inquiry, 46*(3), 289-324.

KIPP Public Charter Schools. (2018). *Focus on character.* Retrieved December 10, 2018, from https://www.kipp.org/approach/character/

Kuh, G. D., Kinzie, J., Buckley, J., Bridges, B. K., & Hayek, J. C. (2007). *Piecing together the student success puzzle: Research, propositions, and recommendations* (ASHE Higher Education Report, No. 32). San Francisco, CA: Jossey-Bass.

Kuh, G. D., Kinzie, J., Schuh, J. H., & Whitt, E. J. (2005). *Student success in college: Creating conditions that matter.* San Francisco, CA: Jossey-Bass.

Light, R. J. (2001). *Making the most of college: Students speak their minds.* Cambridge, MA: Harvard University Press.

Lobo, B. J., & Burke-Smalley, L. A. (2018). An empirical investigation of the financial value of a college degree. *Education Economics, 26*(1), 78-92.

Mayhew, M. J., Rockenbach, A. N., Bowman, N. A., Siefert, T. A., Wolniak, G. C., Pascarella, E. T., & Terenzini, P. T. (2016). *How college affects students: 21st century evidence that higher education works.* San Francisco, CA: Jossey-Bass.

Nagaoka, J., Farrington, C. A., Roderick, M., Allensworth, E., Keyes, T. S., Johnson, D. W., & Beechum, N. O. (2013). Readiness for college: The role of noncognitive factors and context. *Voices in Urban Education, 38*, 45-51.

National Center for Education Statistics (NCES). (2018, November 15). *Achievement gaps.* Retrieved from https://nces.ed.gov/nationsreportcard/studies/gaps/

Ost, B., Pan, W., & Webber, D. (2018). The returns to college persistence for marginal students: Regression discontinuity evidence from university dismissal policies. *Journal of Labor Economics, 36*(3), 779-805.

Partnership for 21st Century Learning. (2015). *P21 framework definitions* [White paper]. Retrieved December 10, 2018, from P21, Partnership for 21st Century Learning: http://www.p21.org/storage/documents/docs/P21_framework_0816.pdf

Perna, L. W., & Thomas, S. L. (2008). *Theoretical perspectives on student success: Understanding the contributions of the disciplines* (ASHE Higher Education Report 34.1). San Francisco, CA: Jossey-Bass.

Peterson, C., & Seligman, M. E. P. (2004). *Character strengths and virtues: A handbook and classification.* New York, NY: Oxford University Press.

Sanders, M. L. (2018). *Becoming a learner: Realizing the opportunity of education.* Plymouth, MI: Hayden-McNeil.

Schreiner, L. A., Louis, M. C., & Nelson, D. D. (Eds.). (2012). *Thriving in transitions: A research-based approach to college student success.* Columbia, SC: University of South Carolina, National Resource Center for The First-Year Experience and Students in Transition.

Sisk, V. F., Burgoyne, A. P., Sun, J., Butler, J. L., & Macnamara, B. N. (2018). To what extent and under which circumstances are growth mindsets important to academic achievement? Two meta-analyses. *Psychological Science, 29,* 549-571.

Sparkman, L. A., Maulding, W. S., & Roberts, J. G. (2012). Non-cognitive predictors of student success in college. *College Student Journal, 46*(3), 642-652.

Steele, C. (2010). *Whistling Vivaldi: How stereotypes affect us and what we can do.* New York, NY: Norton.

Strayhorn, T. L. (2012). *College students' sense of belonging: A key to educational success for all students.* New York, NY: Routledge.

Upcraft, M. L., Gardner, J. N., & Barefoot, B. O., & Associates. (Eds.). (2005). *Challenging and supporting the first-year student: A handbook for improving the first year of college.* San Francisco, CA: Jossey-Bass.

Walton, G. M., & Cohen, G. L. (2011). A brief social-belonging intervention improves academic and health outcomes of minority students. *Science, 331,* 1447-1451.

Yeager, D. S., Romero, C., Paunesku, D., Hulleman, C., Schneider, B. L., Hinojosa, C., ... Dweck, C. S. (2016). Using design thinking to improve psychological interventions: The case of the growth mindset during the transition to high school. *Journal of Educational Psychology, 108*(3), 374-391. http://doi.org/ggb7t2

Yeager, D. S., & Walton, G. M. (2011). Social–psychological interventions in education: They're not magic. *Review of Educational Research, 81*(2), 267-301.

Chapter 1

A Rose by Any Other Name: A Common Language for Understanding Learning Mindsets

Doug Daugherty and Tim Steenbergh

James's Learning Mindset Story: Why Belonging, Growth Mindset, and Resilience Matter

As he laid brick near the university baseball field on a hot July morning, James was in the midst of a remarkable transformation. He could not have imagined the road ahead. David, his boss and mentor, approached him as he prepared to break for lunch. "I want you to go to that admissions office over there on your lunch break," David said. "Tell them you want to take classes here."

The directive surprised James, though he had talked about college with David before. But *this* school? James was Black and 28. The students at this university were predominantly White and in their late teens and early 20s. Also, James was in the early stages of recovery from alcohol and drug addiction.

Ron was friendly and seemed genuinely interested when James walked into the admissions office. James shared openly about his journey and staying clean from drugs, a transparency nurtured by 12-step meetings. Ron listened intently, then asked James to take a placement test—and for permission to share James' story with the admissions committee. James expressed an interest in two majors the university offered: addictions counseling and criminal justice. Ron said he would see what he could do.

Two months later, James was sitting in his first class. He was the only student of color and the only one over 25. Later, he recalled, "It felt like I stepped into a different world. There were lots of doubts." James shared those doubts with his Alcoholics Anonymous (AA) home group, and they told him, "You're supposed to be there. God has you right where he wants you." "Really?" James thought. Years ago, he had dropped out of college. Now he felt overwhelmed by the assignments and technology at his new university. His doubts grew.

In this chapter, we focus on several concepts important for student success: social belonging, growth mindset, resilience, and grit. We use a number of stories to illustrate these concepts. Ample research and our own observations show that successful students are gritty, feel at home in the learning environment, believe they can get smarter, and overcome a variety of challenges. Although we believe the concepts are universal, the particulars of each story are unique and limited. We invite readers to focus on these concepts and look for application within their own classrooms. Many factors influence student success, and we have chosen to focus on those that seem especially practical and enjoy empirical support.

How to Talk About Student Challenges in Higher Education

Research suggests the best predictor of college persistence among Black students is the magnitude of doubt about fitting in at school (Yeager et al., 2016). James's situation was not unique. Doubts about one's intellectual abilities and social belonging are common among college students, not just Black students. However, these doubts are often most pronounced among minority and first-generation college students (Yeager et al., 2016).

How do we discuss the psychological, social, and academic challenges that students like James face? Over the years, much research has focused on the development of academic skills (Dunlosky, Rawson, Marsh, Nathan, & Willingham, 2013; McKeachie, Pintrich, & Lin, 1985; Weinstein, 1989). More recently, however, interest in psychological factors, specifically noncognitive factors, has increased. The term noncognitive differentiates social–psychological–motivational factors from academic, or cognitive, ones. Although the term is awkward, because social–psychological–motivational factors are more generally construed as involving cognition, it helped to create an early language for these important psychological factors, which could then be targeted in efforts to promote student success.

Fortunately, the language has evolved. Noncognitive factors have given way to academic and learning mindsets (Dweck, 2006), which can be defined as the way students think about themselves as learners and the learning environment (Dweck, Walton, & Cohen, 2014). Mindset is the lens through which students interpret their academic and social experiences, form ideas about their capacity to succeed in college, and understand the value of college success. For example, students ask themselves, "Why did my teacher mark up my essay and recommend a rewrite?" "What did my roommate mean by that?" or "Why didn't anybody acknowledge me when I walked into class?" Learning mindset has become interchangeable in discussions of the more generic psychological or motivational factors thought to shape student success.

Another vital question we should ask ourselves as educators and student affairs leaders is, "What are we doing to impact student motivation?" Since the early 1990s, William Miller at the University of New Mexico has transformed the way we think about client motivation in the field of addictions (Miller & Rollnick, 2002), suggesting a client-centered approach to enhancing motivation rather than a confrontational one. Miller's motivational interviewing approach (Miller & Rollnick, 2002) is a way of interacting with people that recognizes the potential to enhance another person's motivation for change, depending on the nature of the interaction. Motivational interviewers seek to build desire for change by expressing empathy, developing discrepancy between an individual's goals and their current behavior, adjusting to resistance, avoiding confrontation, and supporting self-efficacy for change

(Wells & Jones, 2018). These motivational principles and associated concepts have been adopted in other areas of health care and, more recently, in education. The bottom line is that motivation is fluid and needs to be treated as a function of the interaction of a person, their environment, and their current goals. Concerns about student success can be mitigated when faculty and staff pay sufficient attention to the role of environmental and personal factors in student motivation. As educators, we have a responsibility to do all we reasonably can to shape the learning environment in ways that help engage and motivate students.

More recently, Yeager and colleagues (2016) have offered the language of lay theory interventions. Lay theory refers to implicit models that help organize our understanding of the world. We are all lay theorists attempting to make sense of our everyday experiences.

Go back to James's story. During the first few weeks of school, James's learning mindsets probably included doubts about his academic capacity as well as concerns about being stereotyped and treated unfairly as a Black male. He had a sense of not belonging at the university, with questions about the attitudes of his classmates and professors. James succeeded in his first semester and ultimately persisted to graduation. Like many students, though, he experienced several critical points along the journey—times when he felt discounted, alienated, and forgotten at the university. At times, he doubted his academic prowess.

In his first year, James questioned whether he was a good fit for college and if the university was a good fit for him. At the same time, he benefited from various strengths and resources. Some were internal, others external, but most were social, interactive, and dynamic. For James and others, the most helpful experiences tend to be interpersonal and recursive. That is to say, some of the most formative experiences for students involve social connections on campus that are prompted and reinforced by adaptive learning mindsets that, in turn, are stimulated by positive social connections. This is something Greg Walton and his colleagues have discussed in addressing student belonging (Dweck et al., 2014; Walton, 2018). Learning mindsets increase the likelihood that students will engage with available university supports (e.g., faculty, tutoring, social clubs). Concurrently, positive experiences with faculty, staff, and other students increase the possibility that learning mindsets and resilience will take hold. James's journey included many crucial conversations and experiences at pivotal junctures. We examine these strengths and conversations to illustrate the importance of student belonging, growth mindset, and resilience.

Social Belonging: The Importance of Mindset

James walked onto campus that first semester as a street-smart 28-year-old, surrounded by naive 18-year-olds from conservative backgrounds. He was a Black student on a predominantly White campus, and in terms of belonging, the odds were stacked against him. Black students at his university did not fare as well as Whites—they earned lower GPAs and saw higher rates of attrition, mirroring national trends (Tate, 2017). James was also a first-generation college student from a low-income household—two more factors that distinguished him from many of his peers and pegged him as less likely to graduate. To no one's surprise, he wrestled with questions about fitting in. James experienced *belonging uncertainty*, a phenomenon that occurs in academic settings for "members of socially stigmatized groups [who] are more uncertain of the quality of their social bonds and thus more sensitive to issues of social belonging" (Walton & Cohen, 2007, p. 82). Unlike his White, traditional-age peers, James was more likely to question his social connections and interpret them as indicative of his poor fit.

Walton and Cohen (2011) have defined social belonging as a basic human need—"a sense that one has positive relationships with others" (p. 1147). Their work demonstrates that James's experience is a common one. Many students struggle to find a sense of social belonging in their first year on campus. For some, especially students from historically underrepresented and marginalized groups, these feelings result in less academic engagement and poorer outcomes (Dweck et al., 2014). Social psychologists tell us these poor outcomes can arise because of stereotype threat, which happens when those from marginalized groups fear that others see them through the lens of a negative stereotype (Steele, 1997; Steele & Aronson, 1995; Tatum, 2017). In Chapter 4, we explore how this process works and the ways in which mindset interventions can help.

James was at risk for struggling with social belonging, but he also had the advantage of being older, with various life experiences that shaped his mindset and made him more resilient. For example, his 12-step recovery groups had taught him that belonging takes time and often forms around a shared sense of purpose instead of surface characteristics. Though James struggled to fit in, he persevered with the knowledge that belonging is a process. Data from experimental and larger-scale studies suggest that helping students develop a social-belonging mindset can dramatically affect outcomes (Walton & Cohen, 2007, 2011; Yeager et al., 2016). For example, Walton and Cohen (2011) found that a one-hour social-belonging intervention had a significant effect on first-year students, especially Blacks, who saw their achievement gap reduced by 50%. This intervention even demonstrated lasting health benefits in students' senior year. In Chapter 2, we outline some of the principles necessary to successfully deliver such interventions for new students on campus, and in Chapter 4 we describe one such intervention that was delivered through smartphones.

James also took the initiative to connect with a few of his White male professors, including one of the authors (Daugherty). When I recall these conversations, what stands out is the extent to which James was willing to speak freely—questioning, clarifying, or challenging ideas discussed in class. Did it matter that I showed an interest in James and made time to meet after class? I think so, but James took the lead in building our relationship. Of course, this is not always the case with first-generation and minority students—we need to be willing to follow *and* lead in order to connect with them.

Looking back, I see that we were each developing a positive racial–ethnic–cultural identity, which refers to the interaction of race, ethnicity, and culture with regard to one's lived experience and identity development (Cross & Cross, 2008; Tatum, 2017). It was important for me to consider the salience of my racial–ethnic–cultural background as well as James's background, including our experiences with privilege and privation. We both benefited from positive experiences with Black and White classmates, acquaintances, and friends. My training as a psychologist had prioritized, or at least helped me acknowledge, the importance of cultural awareness, the reality of discrimination, and the value of cultural responsivity. Fortuitously, James and I also benefited from our travel together with other students from our rural Indiana campus to Chicago. Perhaps especially meaningful, our time in Chicago involved interacting with many educated professionals of color and celebrating the accomplishments of members of the diverse community.

Intersectionality refers to social vulnerabilities compounded when class, race/ethnicity, gender, nationality, and/or sexuality intersect with regard to the experience of discrimination (Collins & Bilge, 2016). Because educational environments are systems of power and privilege, we need to contemplate how our own assumptions operate at the intersection of identities and the school environment. Moreover, we need to be aware of how our multiple identities, those of our students, and the intersection of these identities shape our work together. Given the disadvantages and stress associated with multiple forms of oppression operating simultaneously, we need to ask, "What mitigating role can educators and mindsets play in an academic context?"

The Importance of Solidarity

James's reflections on belonging in college highlight another important development in his adjustment. The only faculty member of color in our division, Lorna (a Black female) made it a point to connect with James during his first semester. She empathized with him, recognizing the importance of connecting minority students to others with shared life (university) experiences. Lorna offered James a place of psychological safety to talk openly about the challenges of being a Black student at a predominantly White institution. She could do this from a place of understanding and authority in a way that I could not. Lorna's understanding and guidance were vital to James's successful adjustment.

I have listened to other students and faculty of color recount pivotal conversations with peers and mentors. What I have heard these students and colleagues recount, over time, is a developing narrative of belonging as they are, with perspectives, strengths, and experiences that are needed in the community. They often summarize along these lines: "I began to see that this place really needs me. I have a lot to contribute, although it can get tiring at times." This mindset shift involves seeing oneself as a person of value, well prepared for the hopes and challenges of a particular community. Frankly, this shift asks much more of minority students than their counterparts. In addition to offering an adaptive lay theory for first-year students (i.e., concerns about fitting in are common), those of us in higher education need to be intentional about providing mentors and places of psychological safety for students, faculty, and staff who are first-generation or ethnically or economically diverse. Ideally, this happens in the context of a campus culture that suggests, "We are all needed here—how else will we learn and thrive in this wonderfully diverse world? We are better together, when everyone is included."

Beverly Tatum (2017) discussed the importance of such connections in her book, *Why Are All the Black Kids Sitting Together in the Cafeteria? and Other Conversations About Race*. Tatum, a psychologist, details the process of racial–ethnic–cultural identity development in adolescence and adulthood, highlighting the vital importance of connecting with others who have shared life experiences. She wrote:

> The developmental need to explore the meaning of one's identity with others who are engaged in a similar process manifests itself informally in school corridors and cafeterias across the country. Some educational institutions have sought to meet this need programmatically with the creation of school-sponsored affinity groups. …
>
> The opportunity to come together in the company of supportive adults allowed these young Black students to talk about the issues that hindered their performance—racial encounters, feelings of isolation, test anxiety, homework dilemmas—in the psychological safety of their own group. (p. 156)

Tatum offered a vital observation and important charge for leaders in higher education. We need to champion places and people of solidarity, affinity groups, for our underrepresented students. Too often, even those in higher education who should know better misunderstand this. The knee-jerk reaction to affinity groups is to see only segregation and division, rather than the developmental needs of students. Some board members, faculty, and others say things such as, "This only separates students and doesn't help us create a unified community." This issue is far more nuanced than such views recognize, however. It is not an either/or situation; we can promote campuswide unity with respect to diversity while recognizing the developmental needs of all students. Opportunities for spending time with culturally similar peers and mentors are essential to forming a positive ethnic–racial identity, navigating potential challenges to belonging and, ultimately, student success.

Factors other than a student's sense of belonging are also important to their success, including the engagement of high-impact educational practices, student values, cooperative approaches in the classroom, and inclusive teaching/curricula. One other important factor, growth mindset, refers to student, faculty, and staff notions about intelligence and student success. We turn our attention to this factor in the next section.

A Look at Growth Mindset

Twelve-step programs like James's suggest that recovery is a growth process lived out daily. James's recovery helped him see himself as a learner. He sometimes tells a funny story about an early directive from his AA sponsor. The sponsor was concerned that James did not see himself as a learner—rather, he was too focused on proving his knowledge and intellectual abilities. So, the sponsor gave James an assignment: "I want you to regularly go to meetings in the next 30 days, and I don't want you to say anything. Just listen. You don't know enough yet to say anything." Although this idea initially made James angry, over time he came to appreciate how it helped him become a lifelong learner who did not have to be an expert on everything. In terms of his recovery, it helped him move from a *fixed mindset* to a *growth mindset*.

Many readers are likely already familiar with Carol Dweck's research on growth mindset. What follows is designed as a helpful review and extension of that knowledge. Students with a growth mindset believe their intellectual abilities can grow through hard work, determination, and the right strategies—in effect, that they can "get smarter" by exercising their minds (Dweck, 2006; Sisk, Burgoyne, Sun, Butler, & Macnamara, 2018). Like runners who want to get faster, they believe talent and ability can grow with focused, effortful work and useful strategies. These students tend to have somewhat better academic outcomes.

On the other end of the spectrum are students who hold a fixed mindset. They believe there is little they can do to influence their intelligence. From their perspective, some people are born smart, and others are not. They assume "either you have it or you don't." So rather than embracing academic challenges as a way to develop their intellectual abilities, these students see them as a way to demonstrate or test their capacities. Instead of seeing such tasks as opportunities for growth, they see them as potential threats that will reveal their lack of ability. As a result, when challenging academic tasks are presented to those with a fixed mindset, they tend to withdraw.

Focusing on performance instead of learning can lead to self-handicapping, a strategy to save face in the context of potential failure by not exerting effort or downplaying the importance of a performance (Jones & Berglas, 1978). Students position themselves to rationalize the failure by reasoning, "I didn't study" or "I don't care about that test." Typically, the student is unaware of the underlying fixed mindset that causes this behavior and, ironically, has the effect of increasing the likelihood of the feared failure experience.

Understanding Where Mindsets Come From

Maria came to the Research Methods course every day focused on learning as much as she could. Consequently, she had her hand in the air more than most—asking for clarification or elaboration, offering ideas, and trying to apply what she was learning. Whereas many students complained about weekly quizzes and obsessed over their grades, Maria seemed preoccupied with what her instructors were talking about. She would occasionally ask why something was marked wrong, but she never asked for an extra point. Over time, I (Steenbergh) acclimated to Maria's style, though I did not fully appreciate it. Her grades were good, but she never made straight *A*s. I wondered whether she was busy with other things or perhaps just lacked the study skills to ace the quizzes. I am embarrassed to admit that the possibility that Maria cared most about learning the material never crossed my mind. In fact, I did not land on that conclusion until a few semesters later, when the scores from our Major Field Test arrived. All of our seniors had taken the national exam, and there at the top of the list was Maria.

How did Maria outperform all of her classmates, including two students with higher GPAs who went on to complete doctoral degrees in very competitive graduate programs? Maria had a growth mindset. Over the course of her senior year, I came to understand how that happened. She was raised by parents who believed in hard work and character formation. They had reinforced these qualities throughout her childhood and involved her in sports and other activities that required hard work and perseverance. Maria had internalized those early lessons about the value of working hard and enlisting effective strategies and followed them as an undergraduate.

Unfortunately, many students do not enter college with a growth mindset like Maria's. Instead, their early interactions with parents and teachers give rise to fixed mindsets that tend to frame their college experience. As educators, it is important to understand the origin of these mindsets so we can reshape them more effectively. Research exploring the development and influence of learning mindsets provides compelling insights to help us better understand and serve college students.

One of the most fascinating studies in this area examined the effects of praise on children (Mueller & Dweck, 1998). In the study, fifth graders completed moderately difficult logic problems, then were randomly assigned to receive praise in one of three ways. Some students received praise for their intelligence, and others were praised for how hard they had worked. A third group received neutral praise that did not reference their ability or effort. After completing the logic problems and receiving praise, all students received another set of very difficult problems on which everyone struggled (i.e., failure experience). They then received a final set of moderately difficult problems to assess their responses to the failure experience.

The results revealed a remarkable difference. Students who were praised for their effort solved 30% more problems than those praised for their ability; they also demonstrated greater persistence and enjoyment in solving more difficult problems. Such results underscore the importance of early educational experiences, among others, in shaping students' mindsets toward education. They also offer insight into the kinds of feedback and messaging that can help reorient students' thinking.

For college students, and particularly those who, like James, enter higher education aware that they are academically underprepared, a fixed mindset can be especially detrimental to academic success. James began college with doubts about his academic ability and leaned toward a fixed academic mindset. As an 18-year-old, he tried college and failed. At 28, he still wondered whether he had the ability to make it on his second try. Doubts about one's academic abilities, when combined with a fixed mindset, can have a significant impact on the way students engage in work required for academic success (Dweck et al., 2014). James's experience of recovery, and his many conversations with professors, helped him develop a growth mindset that benefited his academic journey. For example, James and I (Daugherty) would occasionally follow up on class with a friendly discussion in my office. Usually, the topic involved theories of addiction, treatment, and recovery. We both wrestled with the balance of lived experience, observations made by experts in the field, research findings, and the complexity of human behavior. We often took turns lobbying for a perspective that we felt was being diminished. We also practiced listening and worked at living (modeling) a growth mindset. Perhaps most important, we gradually acknowledged how these discussions were meaningfully connected to our own stories, our evolving personal/professional identities, and our aspirations.

Resilience and "Everyday Magic"

Resilience is best understood as a dynamic process that exists on a continuum for all of us (Luthar, Cicchetti, & Becker, 2000). Like growth mindset, resilience is fluid, not fixed. It is not something we have or do not have—it is not a trait. Rather, resilience involves mindsets, behaviors, and resources that can be cultivated and developed, but it also entails a sense of self as someone who recovers from setbacks. Resilience has been defined as "the process of adapting well in the face of adversity … it involves bouncing back or steering through difficult experiences. Resilience is also an ongoing process that requires time and effort" (APA, 2011; Masten, 2014). The Academic Resilience Consortium (n.d.), a Harvard University-based group interested in fostering resilience in the college context, characterized resilience as involving "capacities for persistence, creativity, emotional intelligence, grit, cognitive flexibility, risk-taking, agency, adapting to change, delaying gratification, learning from failure, and questioning success." Brooks (2006) complemented these definitions, adding, "Resilience is an ecological phenomenon. It cannot be developed by sheer willpower within the at-risk person; it is developed through interaction within the environment—families, schools, neighborhoods, and the larger community" (p. 70).

Adversity is the soil in which resilience grows. For some students, adversity comes primarily by way of academically challenging coursework. For others, the financial cost of their education threatens to derail them. Still others face significant interpersonal pain as they navigate mental or physical health issues, the death of a loved one, or challenging family situations that occur during college. Whatever the cause, adversity is the context in which we recognize resilience. In the following story, note the interplay between adversity and resilience and between goals and grit.

Lopepe ("Low-peep") Lomong was 6 when he was abducted from his small village in South Sudan. Despite his name, which means "fast" in Swahili, the young boy could not outrun the rebel soldiers who snatched him from his family during Sunday Mass and led him away with other church boys. Like so many of the Lost Boys of Sudan orphaned or displaced during the Second Sudanese Civil War, Lopepe faced terrible conditions. Too young and too small to be trained as a child soldier, Lopepe remained captive in a small hut, where he received little food or water. In the ensuing weeks, he often awoke to find other boys lying still on the floor, having died in the night from malnutrition. In his autobiography, *Running for My Life*, Lopepe tells of the fateful night he and three other boys escaped their makeshift prison and made their way across the African plain (Lomong & Tabb, 2012). For three nights, they ran continuously, stopping during the day to hide from rebel soldiers. Exhausted, they crossed the border into Kenya and were taken to the Kakuma refugee camp, where Lopepe lived with thousands of other Lost Boys for the next 10 years.

Refugee life presented more challenges. Lopepe often spent his days sifting through garbage to find food, anticipating Tuesdays when aid workers would leave their garbage at the dump, and dreaming of Christmas and Easter when he and the nine other boys in his tent would share a chicken. But his greatest joy was soccer. He was fast, and he could handle the ball. As he grew older, Lopepe was required to run around the perimeter of the camp before he was allowed to play—a rule the older boys established to limit how many were on the field. Undeterred, Lopepe covered the 18-mile circumference of the camp each day, without shoes or water.

Although Lopepe loved soccer, it was watching an Olympic race that inspired him to accomplish great things. On the floor of a farmer's home, five miles outside the refugee camp, he sat in front of the first television he had ever seen and watched American sprinter Michael Johnson win Olympic gold in the 400-meter dash. Walking back to camp that night, Lopepe recalled, "I knew that someday, I, too, would run in the Olympics. I did not know how, but I knew I would" (Lomong & Tabb, 2012, p. 57).

Lopepe's story only gets better. After 10 years in the refugee camp, he was brought to the United States by a couple who wanted to give him a better life. Lopepe entered 10th grade at Tully High School in New York, where he joined the track and cross-country teams. His tenacity and previous preparation allowed him to stand out, pacing those teams and eventually winning a state championship. In addition to offering Lopepe a new life, his adoptive parents instilled in him goals that went beyond his dream to compete in the Olympics, as his mother insisted that he attend college. Competing at Northern Arizona University (NAU), Lopepe went on to become the NCAA Division I national indoor champion in the 3,000-meter run and the outdoor champion in the 1,500-meter run. More important to his mother than those titles, however, was the bachelor's degree he would earn at NAU.

It is easy to write off Lopepe's story of resilience as a miracle or a statistical outlier. No doubt, there are good reasons to see it this way, but in doing so, we may fail to appreciate the ubiquitous human capacity for resilience. Although research now suggests resilience is best understood as ordinary rather than extraordinary, this idea runs contrary to early assumptions. Prior to the 1970s, researchers who studied risk factors in childhood expected to find poor long-term outcomes (Garmezy, 1974; Luthar, Cicchetti, & Becker, 2000; West & Farrington, 1973). They were surprised to observe positive outcomes for some at-risk children. At the time, these children were recognized as "superkids" because, like Lopepe (now Lopez), they overcame great adversity. As it turns out, that term was a misnomer, as relatively good outcomes are more common than rare. By and large, human beings are remarkably resilient (Masten, 2014).

Masten's (2014) research suggests that resilience is ordinary, not extraordinary; it is *everyday magic*. Humans are designed to steer through, adapt, persist, and overcome. Masten said that resilience arises from ordinary resources and processes, such as a parent who offers unconditional love and support, or a caring neighbor who stays involved in the life of a child at risk. Resilience is also mediated by psychological processes: the belief that grandmother will always be a source of love (secure attachments), hope for a better future after high school (optimism), plans for dealing with the class bully or the current challenges in geometry (problem-solving skills), and active avoidance of delinquent peers (active coping strategies). The belief that personal choices, actions, and efforts are important to one's future is particularly important to resilience in the face of adversity (Masten, 2014). Our students need to know that resilience is possible and within their developmental–communal reach, and they need to see themselves as resilient. We can build supportive campus communities that bolster and celebrate resilience, starting with acknowledging the mental health needs of our students, without viewing them as damaged and incapable. This is an essential part of growth mindset. Students and their situations are often complicated, even heartbreaking, but students are also incredibly resilient.

Where Grit Fits In

The concept of grit has received much attention, thanks to Angela Duckworth and her book *Grit: The Power of Passion and Perseverance* (2016). She argued that grit is passion and perseverance for long-term goals, as opposed to resilience, which involves positive adaptation in response to stress or setbacks. Grit involves consistent interest in a particular goal and a willingness to persevere to achieve that goal.

Duckworth (2016) acknowledged the importance of growth mindset, locating optimistic self-talk under the grit umbrella. Self-talk comprises internal, often repetitive cognitions, perceptions, and subjective meanings that reflect our take on things and influence how we experience and engage the world. She suggested grit depends on expectations that our efforts can be improved (i.e., growth mindset), yielding better outcomes. We appreciate Duckworth's observation that words are one way to cultivate growth mindset, but modeling it may be most important. We also agree with Duckworth in affirming the basic idea that people really can change.

Importantly, resilience and grit are not the same thing—they manifest themselves in distinct contexts. With resilience, the context is adversity; with grit, it is goal pursuit. We can see this distinction in Lopepe's story. He faced great adversity while imprisoned in South Sudan and later in the refugee camp, but his adversity did not stop there. He had to adapt to the language and culture of the United States and eventually transition to college. His ability to bounce back repeatedly from setbacks and to steer through difficult circumstances allowed him to flourish. But grit took him further. His inherited dream to get a degree propelled him through the challenges and setbacks of college, and his boyhood dream to one day represent the United States in the Olympics carried him through grueling workouts over several years. As his story illustrates, resilience and grit often work in tandem to foster success.

Grit, as measured by brief questionnaires such as Duckworth's Grit Scale (Duckworth, n.d.) or tethered to persistence of cocurricular participation, has been correlated with achievement among diverse groups, from inner-city middle schoolers and affluent college preparatory students to spelling bee finalists and West Point cadets (Duckworth, 2016). There is no doubt that grit has intuitive appeal—particularly in a society that emphasizes meritocracy—but it is not without criticism (Credé, Tynan, & Harms, 2017; Fosnacht, Copridge, & Sarraf, 2017). A recent meta-analysis of 73 grit studies involving more than 66,000 participants indicated only a modest correlation between grit and academic outcomes (Credé et al., 2017). As it turns out, however, there are more nuances to the story. When the researchers looked more closely at both components of grit, they found that academic outcomes had a weak relationship with passion but a much stronger link to perseverance. It seems that passion or sustained interest is not sufficient to achieve positive outcomes. In fact, Duckworth (2016) addressed this, noting that much of grit is perseverance while adding, "Nobody works doggedly on something they don't find intrinsically interesting" (p. 106). Regarding fanning the flame of interest to cultivate a passion (and future persistence), she added that "before hard work comes play" (p. 106).

Grit is inversely correlated with socioeconomic status and opportunities for participation (Duckworth, 2016; Fosnacht et al., 2017). In other words, those who have fewer economic, educational, and other kinds of opportunities tend to score lower on measures of grit. This should come as no surprise. When our students' social, educational, and economic realities place barriers to goal attainment, passion and perseverance naturally diminish. This raises a question that those of us in higher education must seriously consider: Does emphasizing grit inadvertently become another means of disparaging the disadvantaged and marginalized?

Like Lopepe, our students need to be resilient in the face of adversity and gritty in pursuit of their academic and vocational goals. Early adulthood is fraught with challenges for students. Finances fall through, family members get sick, and romantic relationships dissolve, but resilient students steer through these challenges with our support. Grit, then, comes into play regardless of whether students face such adversity. To succeed in college, students must attend classes, read, study, and write, all while limiting activities that offer more short-term enjoyment at the cost of long-term goal attainment. Gritty students are willing to make these sacrifices. As Jerry Pattengale, author of the *Purpose-Guided Student* (2010), says, "The dream needs to be stronger than the struggle" (p. 10)."

Other Examples of Resilience

Resilience comes in many forms. Revich and Shatte (2002) described four major types: overcoming, bouncing back, steering through, and flourishing. A few illustrations support this point. Poet and writer Maya Angelou (2002) shared her story of overcoming a difficult childhood in her book *I Know Why the Caged Bird Sings*. As a child, Angelou was rejected by her mother and brutally raped by her mother's boyfriend. Her childhood was a painful journey through poverty, loneliness, racism, and profound disadvantage, yet she became a widely acclaimed author and a national treasure. Readers may recall her poetry reading at President Bill Clinton's inauguration. Angelou's story reminds us of the human soul's remarkable resilience, with even the most tragic childhood cage being supplanted by a beautiful song.

Sheryl Sandberg, Facebook's chief operating officer, shared her story of bouncing back in the book she co-authored with Adam Grant, *Option B: Facing Adversity, Building Resilience, and Finding Joy* (2017). After her husband Dave Goldberg's unexpected death, Sandberg felt as though she were falling into a bottomless void of despair. She questioned her capacity to persevere, let alone support her children through their grief. Grant, a psychologist, emphasized to Sandberg that although we cannot control what happens to us, we can control how we respond. Little by little, Sandberg regained hope. She illustrated her recovery by recalling a particular milestone:

> We were talking about options for an upcoming father–son activity, and [tearfully] I said that 'I want Dave to go.' [Adam listened] and said, 'Well, option A is not available—so let's just kick the s--- out of Option B." (p. 13)

As Sandberg noted, in some sense, we are all living Option B.

Our guess is that most readers are steering *through* their weeks. (They might also be in the process of overcoming, bouncing back, and/or flourishing.) There are challenges at work, bills to pay, and family members who need our attention and care, as well as a multitude of other concerns. For example, while writing, I (Daugherty) am aware of budget challenges at my university, a deadline for the draft of a book chapter, the need to clarify plans for an upcoming holiday weekend, questions for my wife and me about our housing situation, and concerns about the direction and escalating political divide in our country. Such is life. We are all learning to steer through.

There is an interesting connection between resilience and flourishing, juxtaposed with post-traumatic stress disorder (PTSD). *Post-traumatic growth* is the idea that people not only recover or bounce back but often demonstrate remarkable growth in response to trauma. Sometimes people find a way forward that's more than healing or the return to a previous adjustment level. Recovery can build momentum and resources for continual growth, which leads to flourishing. Flourishing involves a holistic view of well-being, encompassing positive emotions, engagement (flow), rewarding relationships, meaning, and accomplishments (Seligman, 2012).

As students learn and grow in character, they build capacity and resources for flourishing. Aristotle (350 B.C./2003) rightly positioned flourishing as the natural outcome of a virtuous life. Ideally, our resilient and gritty students not only overcome, bounce back, and steer through but also are growing in character and virtue, which is necessary for flourishing. We emphasize learning in terms of knowledge, skills, and attitudes while also tethering it to good character, hence the mission and vision statements of our various institutions. As Dalton and Crosby (2012) noted in their essay on developing character, "The cultivation of moral values and ethical behaviors in undergraduate education has become a persistent and widespread activity in almost all types of higher education institutions" (p. 1). This is rightly so, because student flourishing—the lofty ideal and pursuit of dedicated administrators, faculty, and staff—can only be achieved through character formation.

Resilience, then, is the process of adapting well in the face of adversity. It is advanced through *realistic optimism, active coping, internal locus of control*, and *social supports* (Masten, 2014). Realistic optimism involves thinking positively about our situations, efforts, and outcomes. We err on the positive side without being in denial. Active coping refers to intentionally taking steps to address a problem; it is often contrasted with emotional coping (e.g., "I just try to feel better about my situation"). Internal locus of control involves the belief that choices, rather than simply luck, fate, or external forces, largely determine one's future. Social supports involve the availability and help of others. Social support includes more than just people available to provide support; it also includes our belief that people are willing to help and that it is OK to ask for help. We think of these as aspects and correlates of learning mindsets, as well as useful actions and helpful resources. Along with these resources,

Table 1.1 summarizes what researchers refer to as the short list of factors associated with resilience in young people (adapted from Masten, 2014).

At this point, readers likely recognize some connections between resilience, growth mindset, and belonging. For example, students with a growth mindset are resilient in the sense that they are more willing to acknowledge failure as an opportunity for learning. They are less threatened by failure and more transparent about it. We love what Stanford University does in this regard, annually celebrating a day for acknowledging failures, called "Stanford, I Screwed Up!" For this event, students gather to celebrate the epic failures in their life through storytelling, comedy, music, video, and other creative means. Interestingly, some acknowledgment of warts, problems, and failures also tends to facilitate belonging, particularly in social contexts that value honesty and genuineness (Yalom & Leszcz, 2015). Many assume the opposite—that people will like them if they reveal only their successes. But consider most people's general reaction to someone who only shares stories of personal promise and success. Successful group therapy or college persistence often results in learning how transparency can facilitate social belonging as well as helping us engage with supports.

Table 1.1
Resilience Factors and Associated Resources

Resilience factors	Resources
Caring relationships Effective caregiving/parenting, mentors, close friends, romantic partners	Significant others Family, peers, other caring adults
Problem-solving skills	Learning, thinking, and problem-solving
Personal agency Self-control, self-understanding, planfulness, emotional regulation	Executive functioning Internal locus of control Self-regulation
Motivation to succeed Self-efficacy	Striving for mastery Sense of effectiveness, learning mindsets
Faith, hope, belief that life has meaning	Spirituality and cultural beliefs
Caring and effective schools	Educational opportunities Inclusive teaching, equity, affinity groups
Caring neighborhoods	Social supports Extended family, alternative caregivers, sense of community, equity/justice

Note. Adapted from *Ordinary Magic: Resilience in Development*, by A. S. Masten, 2014. Copyright 2014 by the Guilford Press.

Conclusion

In closing this first chapter, we emphasize a caution about mindsets. Some fear that focusing on mindsets implies that we attribute all shortcomings in education to students, who are somehow broken. We share this fear and want to be clear that nothing could be further from our intent. Focusing on the mindsets of those who are oppressed can be a slippery slope. We recall the words prominently displayed on the website of Claude Steele, the distinguished social psychologist: "If you want to change the behaviors and outcomes associated with social identity, don't focus on changing the internal manifestations of the identity. Focus instead on changing the contingencies to which all of that internal stuff is an adaptation." In other words, mindset interventions can help students, but they are only part of the story. The primary story involves institutional histories, messages, and practices (contingencies) that marginalize students of color and other minority groups. We have more to say about this in Chapter 4.

The focus of this book is on what we as educators can do to engage students and foster more adaptive mindsets among students, faculty, and staff to benefit students and communities. We want to emphasize our belief that personal (mindset) *and* environmental (cultural) changes are necessary. Efforts on both fronts need to work in tandem to maximize the potential for student success. Those of us in higher education must work for institutional change as well as mindset change. Institutional change is important but slow. As a practical matter, we can do much immediate good for students by addressing mindsets. So, we work as allies to do both—promoting student success using mindset interventions and simultaneously addressing institutional change. We can encourage wise interventions that foster adaptive shifts in mindsets as well as necessary environmental changes in schools. Much work is needed to expand access, equity, and opportunity for all students. Mindset interventions are one practical way to move the ball forward: progress, not perfection.

Campus Conversations

The following questions are provided to begin conversations with key players on campus and can be used as starting points for implementing change:

- To what extent do students on our campus feel like they belong? In what areas on campus is belonging emphasized?

- Parker Palmer (2017) has suggested that we teach who we are. To what extent do faculty, staff, and administrators hold a growth mindset that shapes our institutional culture? What would it look like for us and our students if we all approached our work with a growth mindset?

- Where are we celebrating grit and/or resilience on our campus?

- How are we doing with viewing students from a holistic perspective that recognizes both cognitive factors and learning mindsets as key variables in student success?

- What institutional changes are needed to foster a more equitable and inclusive learning environment for students, faculty, and staff?

Next Steps

The following steps are suggestions for moving from exploration to action:

1. Think of a student or colleague who best embodies aspects of the learning mindsets described in this chapter. Send them an email expressing your gratitude for their example.

2. Talk with a student or colleague whose resilience you admire. What type(s) of resilience has this person demonstrated? Share with them what you've observed that demonstrates resilience.

3. List three skills in your life that are important to you (e.g., relating with others, performing at work, playing golf) and then rate the extent to which you hold a fixed or growth mindset about those skills, using a 1 to 10-point scale (0 = *That's just how it is, I can't change*; 10 = *I strongly believe that with hard work I can improve in this area*). Then list the ways in which your view influences how you approach challenges in those areas.

4. Tell a colleague about what you have learned from this chapter and ask them to check in with you next week to see what else you are learning.

References

The Academic Resilience Consortium. (n.d.). Home. Retrieved from https://academicresilience.org

American Psychological Association. (2011). *The road to resilience*. Retrieved from http://www.apa.org/helpcenter/road-resilience.aspx

Angelou, M. (2002). *I know why the caged bird sings*. New York, NY: Random House.

Aristotle. (2003). *The Nichomachean ethics* (J. A. K. Thomson, Trans.). New York, NY: Penguin Books. (Original work published 350 BC)

Brooks, J. E. (2006). Strengthening resilience in children and youths: Maximizing opportunities through the schools. *Children and Schools, 28*(2), 69-76.

Collins, P. H., & Bilge, S. (2018). *Intersectionality*. Cambridge, United Kingdom: Polity.

Credé, M., Tynan, M. C., & Harms, P. D. (2017). Much ado about grit: A meta-analytic synthesis of the grit literature. *Journal of Personality and Social Psychology, 113*(3), 492-511.

Cross, W. E., & Cross, T. B. (2008). Theory, research, and models. In S. M. Quintana & C. McKown (Eds.), *Handbook of race, fascism, and the developing child* (pp. 154-181). Hoboken, NJ: Wiley.

Dalton, J. C., & Crosby, P. C. (2012). Core values and commitments in college: The surprising return to ethics and character in undergraduate education. *Journal of College and Character, 12*(2), 1-4.

Duckworth, A. (n.d.). *Grit scale*. Retrieved from https://angeladuckworth.com/grit-scale/

Duckworth, A. (2016). *Grit: The power of passion and perseverance*. New York, NY: Simon and Schuster.

Dunlosky, J., Rawson, K. A., Marsh, E. J., Nathan, M. J., & Willingham, D. T. (2013). Improving students' learning with effective learning techniques: Promising directions from cognitive and educational psychology. *Psychological Science in the Public Interest, 14*, 1, 4-58.

Dweck, C. S. (2006). *Mindset: The new psychology of success* (2nd ed.). New York, NY: Random House.

Dweck, C. S., Walton, G. M., & Cohen, G. L. (2014). *Academic tenacity: Mindsets and skills that promote long-term learning*. Retrieved from http://k12education.gatesfoundation.org/resource/academic-tenacity-mindsets-and-skills-that-promote-long-term-learning/

Fosnacht, K., Copridge, K., & Sarraf, S. (2017, November). *Peering into the black box of grit: How does grit influence the engagement of undergraduates?* Paper presented at the annual meeting of the Association for the Study of Higher Education, Houston, Texas.

Garmezy, N. (1974). The study of competence in children at risk for severe psychopathology. In E. J. Anthony & C. Koupernik (Eds.), *The child in his family: Children at psychiatric risk*. Oxford, England: Wiley.

Jones, E. E., & Berglas, S. (1978). Control of attributions about the self through self-handicapping strategies: The appeal of alcohol and the role of underachievement. *Personality and Social Psychology Bulletin, 4*, 200-206.

Lomong, L., & Tabb, M. (2012). *Running for my life: One lost boy's journey from the killing fields of Sudan to the Olympic Games*. Nashville, TN: Thomas Nelson.

Luthar, S. S., Cicchetti, D., & Becker, B. (2000). The construct of resilience: a critical evaluation and guidelines for future work. *Child Development, 71*(3), 543-562.

Masten, A. S. (2014). *Ordinary magic: Resilience in development*. New York, NY: Guilford Press.

McKeachie, W. J., Pintrich, P. R., & Lin, Y. (1985). Teaching learning strategies. *Educational Psychologist, 20*(3), 153-160. http://doi.org/bg6z2f

Miller, W. R., & Rollnick, S. (2002). *Motivational interviewing: Preparing people for change* (2nd ed.). New York, NY: Guilford Press.

Mueller, C. M., & Dweck, C. S. (1998). Praise for intelligence can undermine children's motivation and performance. *Journal of Personality and Social Psychology, 75*(1), 33-52.

Palmer, P. J. (2017). *The courage to teach: Exploring the inner landscape of a teacher's life* (20th anniversary ed.). San Francisco, CA: Jossey-Bass.

Pattengale, J. (2010). *The purpose-guided student: Dream to succeed*. New York, NY: McGraw-Hill.

Revich, K., & Shatte, A. (2002). *The resilience factor: Seven essential skills for overcoming life's inevitable obstacles*. New York, NY: Broadway Books.

Sandberg, S., & Grant, A. (2017). *Option B: Facing adversity, building resilience, and finding joy*. New York, NY: Knopf Doubleday.

Seligman, M. (2012). *Flourish: A visionary new understanding of happiness and well-being.* New York, NY: Free Press.

Sisk, V. F., Burgoyne, A. P., Sun, J., Butler, J. L., & Macnamara, B. N. (2018). To what extent and under which circumstances are growth mind-sets important to academic achievement? Two meta-analyses. *Psychological Science, 29*(4), 549-571.

Steele, C. M. (n.d.). Claude M. Steele [Personal website]. Retrieved from https://claudesteele.com/

Steele, C. M. (1997). A threat in the air: How stereotypes shape intellectual identity and performance. *American Psychologist, 52*(6), 613-629.

Steele, C. M., & Aronson, J. (1995). Stereotype threat and the intellectual test performance of African-Americans. *Journal of Personality and Social Psychology, 69*(5), 797-811.

Tate, E. (2017, April). Graduation rate and race. *Inside Higher Ed.* Retrieved from https://www.insidehighered.com/news/2017/04/26/college-completion-rates-vary-race-and-ethnicity-report-finds

Tatum, B. D. (2017). *"Why are all the Black kids sitting together in the cafeteria?" and other conversations about race.* New York, NY: BasicBooks.

Walton, G. M., & Cohen, G. L. (2007). A question of belonging: Race, social fit, and achievement. *Journal of Personality and Social Psychology, 92*(1), 82-96.

Walton, G. M., & Cohen, G. L. (2011). A brief social-belonging intervention improves academic and health outcomes of minority students. *Science, 331*(6023), 1447-1451.

Walton, G. M. (2018, August). *Academic mindsets and "wise" interventions to bolster belonging and growth in college.* Faculty retreat, Indiana Wesleyan University, Marion, IN.

Weinstein, C. E. (1989). Helping students develop strategies for effective learning. *Educational Leadership, 46*(4), 17-19.

Wells, H., & Jones, A. (2018). Learning to change: The rationale for the use of motivational interviewing in higher education. *Innovations in Teaching and Education International, 55*, 111-118.

West, D. J., & Farrington, D. P. (1973). *Who becomes delinquent?* (Second Report of the Cambridge Study in Delinquent Development). London, England: Heinemann.

Yalom, I. D., & Leszcz, M. (2015). *The theory and practice of group psychotherapy.* New York, NY: Basic Books.

Yeager, D. S., Walton, G. M., Brady, S. T., Akcinar, E. N., Paunesku, D., Keane, L., ... Dweck, C. S. (2016). Teaching a lay theory before college narrows achievement gaps at scale. *Proceedings of the National Academy of Sciences, 113*, E3341-E3348. http://doi.org/f8rvsz

Chapter 2

The Implications of Learning Mindsets for the First-Year Experience and Other Key Transitions

Bryce Bunting

Anna and Lori's Learning Mindset Stories: A Tale of Two Transitions

Anna and Lori were quite similar—both first-year students, academically well prepared, and first-generation Latinx. Like nearly all new students, they encountered challenges during their first year. But one felt successful and optimistic at the end of her first semester, and the other was not sure she would even be back for Year 2. What made the difference? Why did one thrive while the other floundered? A closer look at Anna and Lori's stories reveals important factors that might explain why students with similar characteristics often have such different experiences.

Anna's Story

At orientation, Anna noticed she was the only Latinx student in her group. Also, nearly everyone else had a parent with them and already knew how to register for classes, pay tuition, and sign up for student insurance, whereas Anna did not. Though she had been excited about starting college, she now felt a little anxious about coming back in the fall.

"I've never seen so many BMWs in one place," Anna told her mom when she moved in a few months later. As she met other new students, it seemed everyone else had majors, career plans, and internships for the next summer. By the end of the first week, she felt like she was falling behind already. She wondered, "Is this the right place for me?"

College algebra lived up to its hype. Although she was doing everything she had been told—"never miss class, take notes, and do the homework"—she was drowning. At the end of September, she took her first midterm, weighed down by anxiety and wracked by thoughts such as "I've never been a math person." She just hoped she would do well enough to justify the hours of work she had put in studying.

She received her midterm grade—"a 67!" Crushed, Anna went straight home, skipping her other classes. The next day she vowed to study twice as hard. She said no to social opportunities, isolated herself in the library, and doubled down on reviewing her notes and rereading material from the textbook. Three weeks later, she took Test No. 2. She scored a 65. What was she to think? She had worked harder but earned an even lower score. In an emotional call home, she remarked, "I guess I'm not as smart as I thought." As the semester went on, she spent more time alone, regularly missed classes, and invested very little effort in studying. She finished the semester on academic warning with a 1.8 GPA.

Lori's Story

During orientation, Lori heard about the Latinas in STEM program and, although hesitant, stopped by to meet the faculty advisor, Dr. Perez. They only talked for five minutes, but Dr. Perez invited Lori to attend the opening meeting later that fall and suggested, almost in passing, that Lori think about getting involved in research.

Lori was expecting a challenge when she returned to start the semester, but past experiences had taught her to work hard and ask for help when she needed it. By the end of the first week, she had joined a chemistry study group, attended the STEM club's opening meeting, and visited Dr. Perez to ask about majoring in chemistry. It was hard, but she was surviving. Three weeks later, she took her first chemistry midterm feeling confident. The results stunned her. "55 percent! I attend class, do the reading, and am in a study group. How could I fail?" Lori did not know what more she could have done to prepare.

The next day, she visited her teaching assistant for help. In a short but helpful conversation, the TA pointed out Lori's mistakes and told her she could use review questions from the textbook to test herself.

Lori's test scores for the rest of the semester were not as high as she hoped, but she could see she was improving. She stayed involved in the STEM club and was invited to join Dr. Perez's research group for the following semester. The fall semester had been long and hard, but Lori went home for the winter break feeling good about her efforts and with ideas about changes she wanted to make in the spring.

Parts of Anna and Lori's stories feel similar; however, the ways they responded to experiences in their first year were different in subtle, yet critical ways. Students' beliefs about learning, challenges, success, and failure play a significant role in their ability to successfully navigate the transitions inherent in the college experience. With this in mind, what can those with responsibility for shaping the new-student experience learn from students like Anna and Lori?

Mindset as a Critical Outcome for the First Year

Beginning college is challenging—students leave the familiarity of home, may be financially independent for the first time, form new relationships, and typically lack good study habits (cf. Kuh, Kinzie, Schuh, & Whitt, 2005; Upcraft, Gardner, Barefoot, & Associates, 2005). In response, institutions tend to do at least two things to help. First, they develop (often long) lists of first-year outcomes describing what students need to know and be able to do in order to have a successful first year. Then, they develop programs, courses, and activities designed to help students achieve these outcomes.

Although there is nothing inherently wrong with this approach, often the list of key first-year outcomes is so long it raises serious questions, including "Can we really do all of this in a single year?" and "Do we have the resources?" For most institutions, these two questions lead to a confrontation with reality, followed by the question "We can't do it all, so where do we start?" In this chapter, we hope to make the case that giving attention to learning mindsets is one of the very best places to start when designing a comprehensive FYE. We even make a bold claim: Supporting students in developing productive learning mindsets may be the single most important outcome for the first-year experience.

We are not actually arguing that the other learning outcomes for the first year (e.g., developing foundational academic strategies, establishing strong and supportive relationships, and being aware of and accessing campus resources) should be disregarded. Instead, we see fostering learning mindsets during the first year of college as a way to shift students' trajectories and place them on a powerful pathway that, across their college experience, leads to fulfillment of these other key outcomes. Concurring with Carol Dweck (2006), perhaps the godmother of learning mindsets, we believe the simple beliefs explored in this book have the potential to permeate every part of a student's experience, particularly when infused throughout a student's first year of college.

In this chapter, readers will find a brief discussion of the role of learning mindsets in first-year transitions, an analysis of the key principles for developing effective mindset interventions, concrete examples of such interventions, and a brief exploration of the role of learning mindsets in college transitions beyond the first year.

Learning Mindsets and First-Year Transitions

Whether they involve moving to a new city, starting a new job, or becoming a parent, transitions leave us feeling vulnerable as we make sense of and adjust to our new situation. College transitions are no different. Students might wonder what it takes to be successful, fear their academic future, discover past strategies are no longer effective, or feel isolated, among other things. The extent to which they have learning mindsets can either mitigate or exacerbate these thoughts and feelings.

One day in early September 2016, I witnessed this during a particularly lively class discussion. The windowless basement classroom did not help students' engagement most days, nor did the 1 p.m. meeting time—when most people's circadian rhythms take a nosedive. It was a small class—just 22 students, most of whom were in their first semester of college. Because of the course's title (Effective Study and Learning), most students expected it to focus exclusively on study skills and strategies. However, I typically spend the first month working to foster productive learning mindsets among students, knowing these beliefs and attitudes drive academic behavior (Farrington et al., 2012).

For class that day, I had assigned my students a reading from Dweck's book, *Mindset* (2006), which introduces fixed and growth mindsets and discusses how they are influenced by our environment and experiences. Dweck pays particular attention to the problematic impact of well-intended, achievement-oriented praise (e.g., "You're so smart," "You're a natural," "You're so gifted") on young people. In an on-the-fly change to my lesson plan, I also shared an infographic that had been featured in a campus press release just a few days prior. The infographic, titled "Our Stellar 2016 Freshman Class," accompanied a feature article extolling the virtues of the college's incoming students, including the impressive average ACT score and high school GPA, the number of students ranked No. 1 in their graduating classes, and the percentage who had participated in fine arts. Although this fairly typical PR message appeals to recruiters, development staff, and parents, it is also problematic messaging about the ideal student and seemed a perfect exemplar of the achievement-oriented praise Dweck critiques.

I asked students about their reaction to the infographic and how they thought it related to the day's reading. What happened next was both surprising and exciting. Hands immediately shot up—which was rather unusual for this class—and I knew I had touched a nerve. Their responses were swift, emotional, even bordering on visceral. A handful of students had clearly seen the infographic beforehand and formed an opinion of it.

As a whole, students said that by highlighting the aggregate achievements of the incoming class, the institution had inadvertently left students with below-average stats feeling like they might not have what it took to be successful there. One particularly passionate student described how she and a friend had spent nearly all night consoling a roommate who, already struggling with doubts about her belonging, was ready to pack up and go home after she saw the infographic. She genuinely believed she would never measure up. The reactions of the students in my class left me uneasy, wondering how deeply that one infographic might have affected other students, especially those already bearing the burdens of self-doubt or fixed views toward learning and success.

Messaging During a Critical Time

As faculty and staff, we habitually praise the virtues of our students; however, we need to be more thoughtful about both *how* and *when* we offer this praise. For first-year students in my class, highlighting achievement in such a heavily quantifiable way, and during the first week of fall semester, was less than ideal because of the subtle message communicated about belonging and success.

Not surprisingly, academic transitions are associated with declines in performance and increasingly negative attitudes toward school and learning (Alspaugh, 1998; Neild & Weiss, 1999). Accordingly, the FYE is critical because new students tend to be both vulnerable to the negative effects of unproductive academic mindsets and open to the possibility of incorporating new and more productive mindsets (e.g., Farrington et al., 2012; Yeager & Walton, 2011). For example, although my students were distressed by the unintended messaging they identified in the infographic, they were open to a more growth-oriented mindset. They consistently reported that this was one of the most impactful aspects of the course—much more so than any of the academic skills or strategies that followed.

Indeed, the FYE might be seen as a critical period (see Robson, 2002, for an in-depth discussion) with transformative potential because of the inherent opportunities for students to deconstruct unproductive learning mindsets, see challenges as a normal part of college, establish a sense of belonging, and develop resilience for the future. By focusing on learning mindsets as a key aspect of the FYE, then, institutions can inoculate students for the remainder of their college experience by equipping them with beliefs, attitudes, and strategies that allow them to transition successfully through the first year and beyond. However, for learning-mindset interventions to be most effective, they must be carefully designed and implemented.

Building Productive Learning Mindsets: Key Principles for Effective Interventions

Because students' mindsets are shaped by years of experience, influencing these beliefs is a tall order. The good news is that small, simple interventions can have powerful effects (Yeager & Walton, 2011). Although evidence suggests interventions can improve both mindset and achievement, more attention needs to be paid to how and why particular interventions are impactful. Additionally, recent scholarship suggests that the impact of mindset interventions is highly dependent on both context and population (Sisk, Burgoyne, Sun, Butler, & Macnamara, 2018). Well-designed interventions can be impactful, but they are not cure-alls and cannot be implemented indiscriminately for all students or in all settings.

Our goal is to provide a theoretically grounded, highly practical set of essential building blocks that can be adapted and reconfigured to develop customized learning-mindset interventions for first-year students at various institutions. The key components of effective learning-mindset interventions include grounding interventions in sound theory, focusing on shifting student beliefs, delivering interventions early in students' experience, actively involving students in interventions, and paying attention to institutional ethos. These components are discussed in greater detail in the sections that follow.

Ground Interventions in Sound Theory

Learning-mindset interventions target the cognitive and emotional processes associated with learning and school. Thus, they are most successful when grounded in sound psychological theory and then adapted for the students and settings where they are implemented. Practitioners, then, must possess both theoretical and contextual expertise

(Yeager & Walton, 2011). This theoretically informed practical knowledge provides (a) a generalized understanding of the ways in which students' thoughts, feelings, and beliefs affect their college experience and (b) insight into how to best implement interventions in local contexts.

Theoretical grounding is particularly critical as interventions are modified, scaled up, or applied in new ways. In contrast, superficial or inaccurate understanding of psychological theory can lead to interventions or practices that are not only ineffective, but harmful (Walton & Wilson, 2018). For example, to guide their institution's efforts to infuse mindset messaging and simple interventions across the first year, campus leaders at Brigham Young University (BYU) formed a student success committee. This diverse group of stakeholders comprised faculty with expertise in counseling and educational psychology, along with staff from the Office of First-Year Experience, academic advisors, and personnel from Enrollment Services. The committee members' task: develop both institutional messaging and first-year interventions to support students in embracing a growth mindset and feeling an increased sense of belonging.

Together, the committee drew upon its members' collective understanding of psychological theory, experience working directly with first-year students at BYU, and familiarity with existing programming to design a coordinated approach to identifying, reaching out to, and supporting at-risk first-year students. This type of collaborative effort, which leveraged the skill and experience of a wide range of campus partners, is a good model for grounding learning-mindset interventions in sound theory while acknowledging the important role of context in shaping such interventions to fit institutions' needs.

Focus on Shifting Students' Beliefs

Although explicit behaviors are the most proximal cause of student success (Farrington et al., 2012), students' internalized beliefs drive these behaviors (Walton & Wilson, 2018). For Anna, thoughts of "I don't belong here" and "Why study? It doesn't make a difference" led her to disengage from school. In contrast, Lori's beliefs that "college is supposed to be hard" and that "the best students ask for help" led her to do things that successful students do.

The most effective interventions should focus on encouraging students to shed unproductive beliefs and adopt new self-theories that move them to productive action. For first-year students, this might include helping them reframe unproductive beliefs (represented in the first column of Table 2.1). If students enter college holding largely productive beliefs (see column 2 of Table 2.1), the challenge may be helping them maintain those beliefs in the face of adversity. Interventions that target these types of beliefs (i.e., nature of transitions, meaning of challenge, sense of belonging) can be indirect but still leave a powerful impact on critical student behaviors, particularly during the first year.

Table 2.1
Examples of Unproductive and Productive Beliefs

Unproductive beliefs	Productive beliefs
"I didn't think things would be this difficult. What's wrong with me?"	"This is new. It's supposed to be hard."
"Oh well. I've never been a good test taker anyway."	"That test really surprised me. I'll need to study a little differently next time."
"This feels impossible. I'm not sure that it's worth my time or effort."	"I've done hard things before. I just need to keep working and give it some time."
"The professor must just not like the way I write. There's not much I can do about that."	"That didn't go as well as I thought it would. I should talk to the TA and see what she recommends for the next essay."
"Everyone else seems like they're doing just fine. This doesn't really feel like the place for me."	"I'm sure I'm not the only one having a hard time—this is just challenging stuff. I should talk to others in class and see if we can work together."

Deliver Interventions Early in Students' Experience

Intervening in the first year leads to powerful long-term gains (Nelson & Vetter, 2012). Adopting a learning mindset is beneficial anytime in college, but first-year interventions offer a greater return on investment because they initiate a virtuous cycle, beginning with students' early adoption of positive beliefs about learning. These new beliefs lead to greater investment in productive academic strategies, which then boosts success (e.g., Walton, 2014; Walton & Cohen, 2011; Yeager & Walton, 2011). Although interventions deployed during the first year are effective, emerging evidence also shows the value of efforts to shift students' learning mindsets before they formally begin their first year.

As part of its Spartan Persistence Program, Michigan State University (MSU) invites prospective students to complete either a growth-mindset intervention or a social-belonging intervention prior to arriving on campus for their two-day summer orientation (those who do not complete it before orientation are given time to do so after they arrive). In the growth-mindset intervention, students first read an article about how they can "build their brain" through repeated practice and overcoming challenges. Then, they respond to a series of reflective questions designed to help them recall times in the past when they adopted either a growth or a fixed mindset. The belonging intervention is similar. It involves students reading stories from experienced students about how they developed a sense of belonging at MSU, then responding to a series of reflective questions. Those students identified as being at elevated risk of not graduating are also assigned to a Spartan Mentor, whose role is to support students in building a sense of belonging. These faculty and staff mentors meet students at orientation and then follow up at key times throughout students' first year, including after their first exam, before breaks, and before financial aid deadlines.

Such interventions do not yield "magical" outcomes for all students (Yeager & Walton, 2011, p. 268), but by pairing a belonging intervention with focused mentor support, the Spartan Persistence Program has led to increases in first-semester GPA for new students at risk of not graduating. The mentoring program by itself seems to have no impact on students' GPA (Stroman, 2018). Additionally, the growth-mindset intervention has led students to take more challenging courses (Stroman, 2018) and has been associated with higher GPAs among Latinx students, both during their first year and across the university experience (Broda et al., 2018). Although research does not yet provide clarity on why certain groups of students respond differently to particular learning-mindset interventions, there is growing evidence that, on the whole, such interventions particularly affect disadvantaged students (Broda et al., 2018; Paunesku et al., 2015; Stroman, 2018; Yeager, Walton, et al., 2016).

The power of first-year interventions is that they set recursive processes in motion that change students' trajectories early on and have a compound effect on engagement, satisfaction, and achievement over time (Yeager & Walton, 2011; Yeager, Walton, et al., 2016). To maximize long-term impact, however, interventions must emphasize the importance of adopting effective strategies, not just well-intentioned hard work (Dweck, 2016; Walton & Wilson, 2018). Mindsets matter, but other factors—seeking and implementing feedback, replacing ineffective strategies with more effective approaches, and seeking help in the face of challenges, for example—also foster success. The sooner this process begins, the more likely students are to reap benefits. Further, intervening early helps to mitigate the threats to belonging that students often experience in relation to the challenges they encounter during their first year (see Chapter 4 for more discussion of these concepts).

Actively Involve Students in the Intervention

The most effective interventions seem to be those that allow students to participate actively in the process (Yeager, Romero et al., 2016). As an example, after introducing a focused mindset message (e.g., challenges are normal, successful students ask for help, brains grow through effort), an instructor could ask students to engage actively with the message by writing a letter to a future new student who might encounter challenges. This activity might require the students to reflect on a time when they worked hard to improve their intelligence or to debate why learning mindsets matter. The key is that students can reflect on the conceptual content of the intervention, make personal connections between these concepts and their own lived experience, and articulate (ideally for an authentic audience) how they might apply such concepts to benefit themselves, their peers, future students, and others.

These interventions are sometimes described as saying-is-believing exercises (Aronson, Fried, & Good, 2002; Walton, 2014; Walton & Cohen, 2011) because they help students see learning mindsets as more relevant, useful, and believable. Examples include asking students to write responses to simple reflective questions (e.g., "When have you had a growth mindset in the past?" "How might asking for help and adjusting your strategies be important as you begin college?"), draft a letter to another student explaining the ability of the brain to grow through effort, and craft their own mindset and belonging stories to share with others in the future. The power of interventions that involve active participation is that they help students internalize mindset messages through advocating for their value with peers. Students who engage in such interventions are much more likely to adopt productive mindsets themselves and engage in the behaviors that flow naturally from these beliefs (e.g., Yeager, Romero, et al., 2016).

Pay Attention to Institutional Ethos

Students' hypocrisy meters tend to be well honed. They typically know when teachers, academic advisors, or others who formally represent the university say one thing and do another. Therefore, learning-mindset interventions should be supported by an underlying institutional culture of growth, belonging, and resilience. Chapter 5 includes an in-depth discussion of the role of institutional culture in supporting students' development, learning, and success. We mention it here, however, to underscore the importance of minimizing the gap between the subtle messages embedded in mindset interventions and the messages conveyed by institutional policies, procedures, and practices.

An In-Depth Look at a Practical Example

We have chosen to highlight the work of David Yeager and a large group of colleagues (Yeager, Walton, et al., 2016) who conducted three experiments, across a variety of institutional settings, aimed at understanding how learning-mindset interventions could be delivered effectively before students arrive on campus. Readers interested in the details of the experiments are encouraged to read the full article, particularly the open-access online appendices.

Recognizing that no one learning-mindset intervention will be appropriate for all contexts, we share this exemplar to illustrate how practitioners might apply the building blocks described in the previous section. As we introduce this particular intervention, we invite readers to keep a few questions in mind:

- On what psychological theory/theories is this intervention based?
- What types of student beliefs or attitudes does the intervention seem to target?

- What role does timing seem to play in the intervention?

- How are students actively involved?

We hope that reflection on these questions and analysis of this particular example will offer readers insights about the sort of interventions that might be most impactful at their institution and with their students. Here, we briefly describe the most salient features common across all three experimental interventions.

All participants attended high-performing, diverse, urban high schools. All were admitted to either a public flagship university or a selective private university and were identified by their high schools as being "college ready." In all, 9,500 prospective first-year students participated in the study, which comprised nearly 90% of the first-year college students across the three participating institutions.

Each of the three interventions was delivered via the web during participants' senior year of high school in the final months before graduation. In one experiment, school staff administered the intervention in classrooms. In the other two, students completed the intervention on their personal computers on their own time. The format of the interventions was similar across all three experiments and included (a) exposure to learning-mindset messages and (b) a saying-is-believing writing task. The interventions were self-directed and required no facilitation or guidance from school staff or researchers. Further, the intervention tasks were brief; students generally completed them in 25 to 35 minutes.

The activities were presented to students as an opportunity to learn from more advanced students about their experiences transitioning into college as well as a chance to share their own transition experiences to benefit new college students in the future. First, students were exposed to learning-mindset messaging through (a) survey results and stories from older students, (b) a scientific article, or (c) both. The second part of the intervention, the saying-is-believing exercise, asked students to write about how messages in the readings could be relevant to or helpful for a new college student. Students were also told that their written reflections could be shared with future students (and exemplary samples were). These experiments tested both a social-belonging and a growth-mindset intervention.

Social-Belonging Intervention

This intervention was intended to debunk the myth that only certain students (e.g., first-generation students, students from disadvantaged backgrounds) struggle to feel like they belong during their first year of college and to emphasize that all students worry about fitting in at first. Additionally, the intervention was designed to illustrate that feelings of belonging grow over time.

In Part 1 of the intervention, students read the results of a survey they were told was given to current college students who had graduated from their own high school and others like it. The survey results communicated two key messages:

- All new students, regardless of race, gender, or any other background characteristics, worry about whether they will belong.

- These worries tend to go away over time as students actively strive to form relationships with others in college (i.e., a lay theory of college transitions, grounded in established psychological theory).

After reading the survey results, students read actual stories from experienced students that conveyed these same messages.

In Part 2 of the intervention, students completed a saying-is-believing exercise by writing two brief essays. In the first, they were asked to reflect on their past experiences with school transitions (e.g., beginning high school) and to use those examples to argue that it is common for nearly all students to be somewhat unsure of whether they belong in college. In the second essay, students wrote about how and why these initial worries would likely decrease over time.

Growth-Mindset Intervention

The purpose of this intervention was to help students adopt a new learning mindset or lay theory of intelligence by conveying that intelligence is a malleable quality that grows through sustained effort, the use of effective learning strategies, and the modification or abandonment of ineffective ones. Similar to the social-belonging intervention, students began by reading content designed to convey the intended messages of the intervention. In this case, however, the content summarized a scientific research article supporting the idea that intelligence can grow. Then, in the saying-is-believing component of the intervention, students wrote essays communicating this idea to future students who might see themselves as "dumb" because of their struggles in school.

Control materials. Students in the control conditions read similar documents (i.e., survey results, stories, research summaries), but these readings focused on students' adjustment to their physical surroundings during the transition to college. Additionally, they completed a parallel saying-is-believing exercise that asked them to write about how and why students might adjust to the physical environment of college.

Results. Describing the detailed findings and results across all three experiments is beyond the scope of this book. Our goal here is to briefly describe the overall findings and themes emerging from the study that hold practical relevance for FYE staff, administrators, and faculty.

Collectively, these three experiments provided strong support for the formal, strategic practice of helping first-year students understand that the challenges in the transition to college are both normal and surmountable. Further, the study demonstrated that, when delivered prior to college matriculation, these messages can improve key first-year outcomes, particularly among disadvantaged students. Specifically, the lay theory interventions were associated with increased persistence through the first year of college (defined as continuous full-time enrollment through the end of the first year) and with improved first-year GPA for students in the experimental conditions, compared with students in control conditions.

Further, analysis of follow-up survey data collected six months after students began college suggested that these positive first-year outcomes among those in the experimental groups were driven largely by higher levels of social and academic engagement. In particular, students who participated in the lay theory interventions were more likely to have (a) had close relationships with friends and mentors in their first year, (b) been involved in extracurricular groups, and (c) sought out and accepted help from on-campus academic support services. In short, students introduced to strategic, institutional messaging around both belonging and mindset are more likely to do the things that lead to success in the first year.

One important disclaimer: Of the two interventions (i.e., social belonging and growth mindset), social belonging seemed particularly powerful. Although the growth-mindset interventions were associated with positive first-year outcomes, this was only true when the growth mindset message was represented as an institutional belief or value. In the experiment in which a growth mindset was represented as a private belief and not part of the institutional culture, students who received that messaging were no more successful than students in the control group.

In short, pre-arrival interventions focused on a growth mindset should make it clear to students that (a) the institution itself endorses a growth mindset and (b) faculty and staff collectively believe students can grow their intelligence through effort and applying effective learning strategies. As important as students' own internalized beliefs around the malleability of intelligence are, absent a complementary institutional growth mindset, these beliefs were not associated with improved first-year success.

Overall, the research on learning-mindset interventions suggests that for maximum impact, they should

- be based on simple lay theories of belonging and growth, emphasizing that feeling out of place is normal and that both belonging and intelligence grow through effort;

- leverage the power of saying-is-believing by requiring first-year students to convey the same messages to future students, drawing on their own past experiences with school transitions; and

- be delivered as early in students' college experience as possible, ideally before they matriculate.

In their study, Yeager, Walton, et al. (2016) disaggregated their results based on students' race and ethnicity, as well as their first-generation status. These analyses demonstrated that interventions that included these features appeared to affect all students positively, with particular benefit for students from underrepresented minority groups and first-generation students.

Learning Mindsets and Transitions Beyond the FYE

In addition to enhancing the FYE, learning mindsets are important for other key transitions in college, including (a) the transition to the sophomore year, (b) the transition to a major or academic program, and (c) the transition from the undergraduate experience to graduate school or a career.

Transition Into the Sophomore Year

The sophomore year is critical to students' development as they move from external to more internal sources of authority (Baxter Magolda, King, Taylor, & Wakefield, 2012). Additionally, students often engage in existential questioning as they grapple with queries such as "Why am I taking these classes?" and "What is the real purpose of college?" (Gahagan & Hunter, 2006). Compounding all of this, students encounter more rigorous advanced coursework, often without the same degree of support they experienced in their first college year.

As with the first year, learning mindsets are crucial as students face the challenges associated with these changes. Further, such mindsets can be important pathways to thriving in the sophomore year, defined as being "fully engaged intellectually, socially, and emotionally in the college experience" (Schreiner, 2010, p. 4). Thus, students who embrace a growth mindset and demonstrate resilience during this time are well positioned to thrive (Schreiner, Miller, Pullins, & Sepelt, 2012). Sense of belonging is also a key factor in this transition and a strong predictor of thriving (Schreiner, 2013).

High-quality academic advising can be another powerful way to support successful sophomore transitions (Schreiner et al., 2012). Skilled academic advisors can work to reinforce messaging around the malleability of intelligence and the importance of persistence, accessing resources, and using effective academic strategies. Further, advisors can be important partners as students seek out majors, involvement opportunities, internships, and faculty-mentoring relationships—all of which bolster students' sense of belonging. Continuing to cultivate this growing sense of belonging is a key developmental task for sophomores, and advisors have an invaluable role in supporting these efforts.

Transition Into a Major

Learning mindsets also shape students' decisions about majors and can lead some students to undermatch with majors that are less meaningful or challenging than those to which they are more drawn but perceive as beyond their abilities. For example, a female student from an underrepresented population might develop an interest in STEM fields in high school. However, a low sense of belonging in college or a fixed mindset regarding her abilities could lead her to pursue a major in a different discipline because of a fear of failure or a belief that she is not cut out for certain STEM programs (e.g., "I've never really been a science person").

In contrast, learning mindsets inoculate students against the disappointment of situations requiring changes to academic plans (e.g., not being admitted to medical school). When these events occur, relationships with mentors who encourage learning mindsets, consistent institutional messaging around mindset, and policies and practices that celebrate growth and resilience are indispensable.

Anyone who works closely with students, whether an advisor, faculty member, or institutional staff, can play an important role in challenging and supporting students to approach academic planning and decisions about majors from a growth standpoint. To do so, it is important to be attuned to *mindset moments* (i.e., times when students experience significant disappointment, loss, or unmet expectations, leading them to change academic plans) and engage students in helpful dialogue, reflection, and reframing of their experiences. During these conversations, be sure to listen closely and observe signs of fixed-mindset thinking or indications of waning sense of belonging as they relate to a student's transition into a major or academic program. If these problematic mindsets become apparent, responding with both empathy and gentle nudges toward growth-oriented ways of thinking is important. Readers might also consider learning more about advising frameworks such as appreciative advising (Bloom, Hutson, & He, 2008) and self-authorship (Baxter Magolda, 2004) to explore skills for engaging in these conversations. Helping students reflect on past successes and encouraging effort-based attribution, effective strategies, and help-seeking can make a tremendous difference as they confront academic challenges and map out their college plans.

Working with colleagues to reinforce messaging around learning mindsets through well-designed media campaigns, strategically planned during registration and course selection periods, can also help. At Stanford University, The Resilience Project (http://resilience.stanford.edu) has used storytelling, campuswide events, ongoing programming around resilience, and academic support resources to develop a culture that not only normalizes failure but celebrates it as an integral part of learning and a shared experience for everyone on campus. Similarly, at High Point University, the campuswide Quality Enhancement Plan includes developing videos, visual displays, and teaching and advising resources that encourage faculty, staff, and students alike to embrace learning mindsets.

The underlying principle of these efforts is that, with learning mindsets, students can respond to inevitable academic challenges with optimism, resilience, and a steadying confidence that they belong. These sorts of mindsets are critical throughout college, but particularly during times when students are making decisions about courses, majors, or limited-enrollment programs. Just like in the first year of college, these decision points are valuable transitional periods during which students benefit greatly from support in adopting learning mindsets.

Transition From College to Career

The post-college transition is receiving increased attention as pressure mounts for institutions to ensure that graduates have the skills and abilities to thrive in the workplace. Learning mindsets are just as important for the transition out of higher education. College career centers can be powerful partners in incorporating learning mindsets into career readiness resources and programming. For example, career advisors can focus on preparing students to articulate (a) how to demonstrate a growth mindset for a variety of audiences (e.g., employers, graduate selection committees); (b) the key experiences that helped them develop a productive learning mindset; and (c) how this mindset affects their day-to-day behavior as well as their future experiences in employment settings. Additionally, as e-portfolios become more common, institutions might consider requiring upper-division students to compile mindset portfolios that include both reflections and artifacts demonstrating the development of productive learning mindsets.

Across these efforts, it is imperative that institutions reinforce the messages discussed throughout this book: the importance of ongoing learning and growth; the normality of struggle; the fact that abilities (academic and otherwise) grow with effort; and the importance of learning from mistakes, failure, and disappointment.

Conclusion

Learning mindsets are critical during times of transition, particularly for first-year college students. We saw elements of this in Anna and Lori's stories. Anna's initial struggles led to doubts about whether she belonged or was capable of succeeding in college. Consequently, she disengaged, continued using ineffective strategies, and sunk deeper into discouragement throughout her first semester. Lori encountered similar challenges, but her mindset—realizing that struggle is normal, ability grows through effort, "smart students" ask for help, and "I belong here"—gave her hope that she could succeed and the motivation to do the things that led to eventual success.

Students' beliefs about learning, challenges, success, and failure play significant roles in their ability to navigate the transitions inherent in the college experience. By supporting students in developing productive learning mindsets, starting this process early, and providing consistent messaging and support throughout the college experience, institutions take important steps in fostering success for all students on their campuses.

Campus Conversations

The following questions are provided to begin conversations with key players on campus and as starting points for implementing change:

- What role do learning mindsets play in existing FYE programming/initiatives?
- Where might learning mindsets play a more prominent role?
- Which stakeholders should be involved in efforts to infuse learning mindsets into the FYE?
- What are the other key transitions for students on your campus? What roles do learning mindsets play in these transitions?
- Which characteristics of the interventions discussed in this chapter could be adapted for your campus?

Next Steps

The following steps are suggestions for moving from exploration to action:

1. Conduct a mindset audit of the FYE (see Table 2.2). How are students supported in developing learning mindsets? Rate the institution's efforts on a 4-point scale (1 = *not at all*, 2 = *somewhat*, 3 = *fairly well*, 4 = *very well*) and describe the reason for this rating.

2. Convene a group of core first-year stakeholders and initiate a dialogue around learning mindsets, using the questions from the "Campus Conversations" section above.

3. Identify one or two potential mindset interventions for the first year. Develop initial plans and share them with colleagues for feedback.

Table 2.2
Mindset Audit

	Growth Mindset	**Belonging**	**Resilience**
Orientation	Rating: Rationale:	Rating: Rationale:	Rating: Rationale:
Advising	Rating: Rationale:	Rating: Rationale:	Rating: Rationale:
Common reading	Rating: Rationale:	Rating: Rationale:	Rating: Rationale:
Residence life	Rating: Rationale:	Rating: Rationale:	Rating: Rationale:
Convocation	Rating: Rationale:	Rating: Rationale:	Rating: Rationale:
First-year seminar	Rating: Rationale:	Rating: Rationale:	Rating: Rationale:
Undergraduate curriculum	Rating: Rationale:	Rating: Rationale:	Rating: Rationale:

Note. Rate how well students are supported in developing learning mindsets across institutional initiatives (1 = *not at all*, 2 = *somewhat*, 3 = *fairly well*, 4 = *very well*).

References

Alspaugh, J. W. (1998). Achievement loss associated with the transition to middle school and high school. *Journal of Educational Research, 92,* 20-26.

Aronson, J., Fried, C., & Good, C. (2002). Reducing the effects of stereotype threat on African American college students by shaping theories of intelligence. *Journal of Experimental Social Psychology, 38,* 113-125.

Baxter Magolda, M. B. (2004). Learning partnerships model: A framework for promoting self-authorship. In M. B. Baxter Magolda & P. M. King (Eds.), *Learning partnerships: Theory and models of practice to educate for self-authorship* (pp. 37-62). Sterling, VA: Stylus Publishing.

Baxter Magolda, M. B., King, P. M., Taylor, K. B., & Wakefield, K. M. (2012). Decreasing authority dependence during the first year of college. *Journal of College Student Development, 53*(3), 418-435.

Bloom, J. L., Hutson, B. L., & He, Y. (2008). *The appreciative advising revolution.* Champaign, IL: Stipes.

Broda, M., Yun, J., Schneider, B., Yeager, D. S., Walton, G. M., & Diemer, M. (2018). Reducing inequality in academic success for incoming college students: A randomized trial of growth mindset and belonging interventions. *Journal of Research on Educational Effectiveness, 11*(3), 317-338. http://doi.org/gf4w8r

Dweck, C. S. (2006). *Mindset: The new psychology of success.* New York, NY: Random House.

Dweck, C. S. (2016, January 11). *Recognizing and overcoming false growth mindset.* Retrieved from https://www.edutopia.org/blog/recognizing-overcoming-false-growth-mindset-carol-dweck

Farrington, C., Roderick, M., Allensworth, E., Nagaoka, J., Keyes, T., Johnson, D., & Beechum, N. (2012). *Teaching adolescents to become learners. The role of noncognitive factors in shaping school performance: A critical literature review.* Chicago, IL: University of Chicago Consortium on Chicago School Research.

Gahagan, J., & Hunter, M. S. (2006). The second-year experience: Turning attention to the academy's middle children. *About Campus, 11*(3), 17-22.

Kuh, G. D., Kinzie, J., Schuh, J. H., & Whitt, E. J. (2005). *Student success in college: Creating conditions that matter.* San Francisco, CA: Jossey-Bass.

Neild, R. C., & Weiss, C. C. (1999). *The Philadelphia Education Longitudinal Study (PELS): Report on the transition to high school in the School District of Philadelphia.* Philadelphia, PA: Philadelphia Education Fund.

Nelson, D. D., & Vetter, D. (2012). Thriving in the first college year. In L. A. Schreiner, M. C. Louis, & D. D. Nelson (Eds.), *Thriving in transitions: A research-based approach to college student success* (pp. 41-63). Columbia, SC: University of South Carolina, National Resource Center for The First-Year Experience and Students in Transition.

Paunesku, D., Walton, G. M., Romero, C., Smith, E. N., Yeager, D. S., & Dweck, C. S. (2015). Mindset interventions are a scalable treatment for academic underachievement. *Psychological Science, 26*(6), 784-793. http://doi.org/cckkmn

Robson, A. (2002). Critical/sensitive periods. In N. J. Salkind (Ed.), *Child development* (pp. 101-103). New York, NY: Macmillan.

Schreiner, L. A. (2010). The "thriving quotient": A new vision for student success. *About Campus, 15*(2), 2-10.

Schreiner, L. A. (2013). Thriving in college. *New Directions for Student Services, 143,* 41-52.

Schreiner, L. A., Miller, S. S., Pullins, T. L., & Sepelt, T. L. (2012). Beyond sophomore survival. In L. A. Schreiner, M. C. Louis, & D. D. Nelson (Eds.), *Thriving in transitions: A research-based approach to college student success* (pp. 111-136). Columbia, SC: University of South Carolina, National Resource Center for The First-Year Experience and Students in Transition.

Sisk, V. F., Burgoyne, A. P., Sun, J., Butler, J. L., & Macnamara, B. N. (2018). To what extent and under which circumstances are growth mind-sets important to academic achievement? Two meta-analyses. *Psychological Science, 29*(4), 1-23.

Stroman, C. (2018, October 25). *Mindsets and the learning environment: Pairing light-touch learning mindset interventions with a long-term campus initiative* [Blog post]. Retrieved from http://mindsetscholarsnetwork.org/mindsets-learning-environment-pairing-light-touch-learning-mindset-interventions-long-term-campus-initiative/

Upcraft, M. L., Gardner, J. N., Barefoot, B. O., & Associates. (Eds.). (2005). *Challenging and supporting the first-year student: A handbook for improving the first year of college.* San Francisco, CA: Jossey-Bass.

Walton, G. M. (2014). The new science of wise psychological interventions. *Current Directions in Psychological Science, 23,* 73-82.

Walton, G. M., & Cohen, G. L. (2011). A brief social-belonging intervention improves academic and health outcomes of minority students. *Science, 331*(6023), 1447-1451.

Walton, G. M., & Wilson, T. D. (2018). Wise interventions: Psychological remedies for personal and social problems. *Psychological Review, 125*(5), 617-655.

Yeager, D. S., Romero, C., Paunesku, D., Hulleman, C. S., Schneider, B., Hinojosa, C., … Dweck, C. S. (2016). Using design thinking to improve psychological interventions: The case of the growth mindset during the transition to high school. *Journal of Educational Psychology, 108*(3), 374-391.

Yeager, D. S., & Walton, G. M. (2011). Social–psychological interventions in education: They're not magic. *Review of Educational Research, 81*(2), 267-301.

Yeager, D. S., Walton, G. M., Brady, S. T., Akcinar, E. N., Panesku, D., Keane, L., & Dweck, C. S. (2016). *Teaching a lay theory before college narrows achievement gaps at scale.* Proceedings of the National Academy of Sciences, USA, 113, E3341-E3348.

Chapter 3

What do Mindset and Belonging Interventions Look Like in the Classroom?

Amy Baldwin

Helen's Mindset Story: When Developing Learning Mindsets Starts With Faculty

Helen earned a doctoral degree in organic chemistry and began her career as an assistant professor at an urban university that serves a diverse student body. When she interviewed, the department chair emphasized the importance of publishing in her field and that although Helen would be assigned introductory courses her first year, she would be expected to help the department increase its productivity and prestige.

Organic chemistry, Helen knew, was not for the faint of heart. Many a high-achieving student of science had damaged their GPAs taking the course. Helen also believed that students who learned the fundamentals of the course could succeed, but she felt too many students did not take the course—and the intensive time required to master the material—as seriously as they should. "If they would come in motivated and ready to learn," she told a senior faculty member in a department meeting, "then my work would be so much easier, and more enjoyable." The course was often the last stop on the fantasy train for students hoping for a lucrative career in the medical field, Helen repeated to her colleagues.

Helen, then, was not surprised when almost half her students failed or dropped the course each semester. Instead of being perplexed or even ashamed by the outcomes, she and her colleagues, especially her chair, believed the course was functioning properly—as a gatekeeper to more difficult courses and eventual careers for which many students were not well suited. "Who wants a nurse, physical therapist, or doctor who cannot master the basic content of science?" Helen often asked.

She was comforted in this thinking when students came by her office to tell her why they had dropped and that the course made them rethink their "naïve" major and career choices, as they put it. Colleagues often told her that students avoided her sections because they knew her reputation: a highly competent chemistry professor with challenging and unbending standards. "Good," Helen would reply. "I only want students in my classes who are up to the challenge and are willing to embrace the difficulty of the course. If they come in with doubts about their ability, I don't want to coddle them."

Helen felt that her department chair valued her research output highly; thus, she was not compelled to rethink her teaching methods. In fact, her evaluations rarely included her teaching outcomes and student evaluations. However, that all changed the day a newly hired provost met with the department about its course completion data and graduation rates. The provost, charged with improving student outcomes because of a legislated formula for higher education funding, noted the high attrition and failure rates in several first-year gateway courses, including organic chemistry. While the provost praised the department's increase in grant-funded research and publications, she asked that the chair and faculty get on board with improving the outcomes of student learning.

The provost shared the new strategic plan adopted by the university's board of trustees, which included improving outcomes for first-generation students and students of color in STEM fields. Reading the data, Helen realized that almost all of her students of color were dropping or failing her classes and that the chemistry department had graduated far fewer first-generation students and students of color than any other major. It was part of the institution's mission, the provost reminded faculty, to serve the students they had, not the ones they wished they had. Helen decided to take some time to rethink her teaching. But where to start?

Assessing Faculty Mindsets

One of the first steps in making change is to consider how one's own behaviors might be affecting current outcomes. An option for Helen, then, was to review her own mindset and behaviors regarding student learning. For example, did she truly believe that through sustained, focused effort, students, even those from disadvantaged backgrounds, could master organic chemistry?

Studies have shown that how teachers view their students can have both positive and negative effects on students' achievement in the classroom (Raudenbush, 1984; Rosenthal & Jacobson, 1968). Yeager (2017), in a talk at the University of Notre Dame, discussed the effect of teachers who implement growth-mindset interventions but inadvertently undermine those efforts through statements or actions that align with a fixed mindset. For example, a professor who praises only students who get the answer quickly is reinforcing fixed mindset rather than encouraging the struggle and time it takes to learn (Yeager, 2017). Although the curriculum and policies of the course might support the tenets of growth mindset, verbal "slip-ups" by faculty often undermine an intervention.

Some research on growth mindset and belonging has focused on classroom outcomes associated with course performance (Paunesku et al., 2015; Yeager & Dweck, 2012; Yeager et al., 2016). Thus, Helen's logical first step toward creating an environment that fostered growth mindset and belonging might involve a classroom climate and course structure that mirrored best practices in the research. For example, she could review her course content and assessments and consider revising them to make them less intimidating.

Before reviewing and revising her course to foster growth mindset and belonging and improve student outcomes, Helen could ask herself some questions:

- How do I demonstrate growth mindset when I am talking to and about students?

- Alternately, how do I demonstrate fixed mindset?

- Where in my course are challenges that most students face, and how do I let them know those challenges are coming and what to do about them?

- What kinds of words, images, and stories that reinforce productive learning mindsets can I share with students throughout the semester?

Additionally, Helen could think about her interactions with colleagues by asking herself:

- How do I speak about students to other faculty and staff?

- What points in the semester are most challenging for me to maintain language that fosters growth mindset and belonging when communicating about students?

By asking these questions, Helen could acknowledge her own tendencies and biases about learning. In fact, during this process, Helen shared with a colleague her frustration with revamping her course after some students still did not improve their mastery of the content. She knew she worked very hard and cared about her students, but she sometimes wondered where the students' responsibilities fell in the learning process.

Confronting our own beliefs about others' learning is not easy, but it can lead to growth and improvement. In Helen's case, it could be a crucial first step. After reviewing her beliefs on student learning and the ways she communicated that message, Helen could then consider changes to her course.

Learning Mindsets in the Classroom

Creating a classroom experience around mindset and belonging gives students the opportunity to learn about and practice prescribed strategies within a defined amount of time. Doing so also allows faculty to assess student understanding and application of learning mindsets and belonging by witnessing student behaviors and performance.

How can faculty incorporate learning mindsets into their courses while helping students develop a sense of belonging? Current studies provide a wealth of examples, not only on what to provide students in terms of mindset interventions but also when and how (Fink, Cahill, McDaniel, Hoffman, & Frey, 2018; Schmidt, Shumow, & Kackar-Cam, 2017). As discussed in Chapter 1, providing students what researchers refer to as lay theories, or beliefs that the college transition and its challenges are normal and not indicative of a lack of promise or belonging, is one strategy to support developing growth mindset in the classroom.

To provide a lay theory of growth mindset, Yeager (2017) suggested sharing with students basic information about brain growth into adulthood and that challenges and setbacks in the learning process are normal and actually help form strong neural connections. In essence, these ideas are the foundation of growth mindset, and just sharing them with students can have a positive effect on outcomes (Paunesku et al., 2015). Schmidt and colleagues (2017) saw gains for ninth graders who received content about how the brain works and were asked to complete other tasks:

> Through structured activities, students [were also] encouraged to identify personal challenges with attention, organization, nutrition, and stress, to make plans to apply what they have learned to address these challenges in the context of their science work, and to reflect upon the efficacy of the activities and strategies they tried. (p. 588)

Because most students "don't do optional," faculty might need to incorporate opportunities for students to reflect on using the principles of brain research to work through challenges in their courses. For example, a reflection question on a quiz, test, or written assignment could ask students to describe how they have used what they know about how the brain learns to complete their work. In Helen's case, she might provide students a short reading on the brain's malleability and an explanation of growth mindset at the beginning of the semester. Then, she might ask them to use that information to do one or more of the following:

- develop a mantra for when they encounter difficult content or course assignments,

- create a plan for working through difficulties, or

- reflect on what works for them and on what they need to change.

Such intentional activities or opportunities for student analysis and reflection can result in the optimal outcome: Focused effort and effective learning strategies improve learning.

Belonging in the Classroom

The underrepresented students in Helen's classes had not been succeeding, and her institution's renewed emphasis on improving student outcomes for minority and first-generation students in STEM disciplines put a spotlight on the outcomes from her courses. Research on belonging provides institutions with concrete strategies to improve outcomes for minority students. Walton and Cohen (2011), in a study designed to test an intervention on minority student academic achievement and well-being, implemented a social-belonging intervention in the form of a narrative read by students. The narrative conveyed that the college transition involves challenges that all students face and are not indicative of potential. The intervention added a saying-is-believing step beyond the narrative:

> Participants were asked to write an essay describing how their own experiences in college echoed the experiences summarized in the survey. They then turned their essay into a speech, which they delivered to a video camera. These materials, participants were told, would be shown to future students to help ease their transition to college. (p. 1448)

The results of the study showed that African American students who received the intervention improved their academic performance, as demonstrated by higher GPAs, as well as self-reported health and well-being over a three-year period.

Helen could implement a social-belonging intervention by providing students with narratives from previous students who overcame challenges in organic chemistry by using a range of strategies and available resources. Helen's current students would receive the message that challenges are a normal part of the learning process, setbacks are temporary, and students can overcome them. To boost this intervention, Helen could ask students to write about their own experiences in getting through challenging courses or to give advice to future students on how to succeed in the organic chemistry class, using information they had learned about mindset and belonging.

In addition to introducing the growth mindset content and sense-of-belonging narratives, faculty can provide opportunities to learn about and reinforce principles of growth mindset and belonging by

- using assessments to evaluate students' disposition to learning mindsets,
- using intentional course assignments that help students anticipate challenges and determine methods of overcoming them,
- using intentional course assignments to address failure or falling short of goals, and
- completing end-of-course and comprehensive assignments that incorporate learning-mindset questions and allow for deep reflection.

When Helen assigns homework problems that have been challenging for her previous students, she could identify where they are likely to struggle and what strategies they could use to answer them correctly. Helen could also ask students to review their graded assignments and describe why they think they may have fallen short of mastering the material. The emphasis in these assignments should be threefold: (a) normalizing the struggle and failure of students to learn organic chemistry, (b) helping students determine what has caused their challenges, and (c) finding effective methods for successfully learning the material.

Although these recommendations seem to point to additional work by faculty and students, they are easy to add to processes already in place. For example, one or two questions on a course final that allow students to reflect briefly on their progress throughout the semester would take little time to add and review.

Another opportunity for faculty comes during what Yeager (2017) called "crises of confidence," or times in which students experience extreme self-doubt of their abilities during a course. For example, Helen identified her course's third unit and its test as a "grade killer" because a third of her class regularly saw a drop of a letter grade upon completing it. Knowing that course averages for even the grittiest students dipped with the third unit, Helen could prepare all of her students for this upcoming challenge by sharing what Yeager (2014) called "everyday phrases" that reflect growth mindset and the process of learning. One example is

> I see all of you working hard, and that's going to pay off. Your grade may not reflect that right now, but in a few weeks, you'll see how your hard work has laid the foundation for the rest of the semester.

She could also reassure students that a grade setback is normal and temporary (e.g., grades normally improve on the next test) by reminding them of the narratives of past students, as described above, or by creating student narratives around this unit.

Here is another statement Helen could make that would help normalize the experience and emphasize the process of learning:

> Most of you should be struggling at this point. You'll find your grade dips a bit, and some of you will worry about that. That's normal. It happens every year. I promise that if you stay engaged and work hard, things will become clearer in the next week or two.

Additionally, Helen could review the tone of messaging in her syllabus and course documents as well as out-of-class communication related to the course. While doing this, she could ask herself questions such as:

- Do the expectations of the course support the principles of growth mindset and belonging? If not, what phrases can convey the expectations that students will be challenged but supported?

- Do the policies on late work, makeup work, and grading reflect an opportunity for students to develop as learners and to weather potential setbacks in mastering the content? If not, what changes could support students who struggle to master concepts and skills?

- What other considerations should I address to support growth mindset and belonging principles? Do the structure of course assignments (e.g., breaking a large project into a series of smaller ones), the weights of assignments as they affect the overall grade, and the evaluation/feedback loop support the idea that experiencing obstacles in learning is normal and that improvement over time is valued?

As we discuss in Chapter 5, creating a campus culture that supports growth mindset, belonging, and resilience requires reviewing messages and materials produced at all levels of an institution. It is similar with communication in the classroom: Faculty should structure their course assignments to support growth mindset and resilience, which can allow students to learn from early mistakes and master skills.

Using Feedback to Reinforce Growth Mindset and Belonging

The cornerstone of any course is the feedback that students receive on written and oral assignments, homework or problem sets, and tests. It is perhaps not surprising, then, that feedback, both formal and informal, can affect students' learning mindsets and sense of belonging. Steele's (1992, 1997, 2010) research on stereotype threat uncovered insights on how students' feelings about themselves can affect their performance, and specifically how critical feedback can affect minority students' sense of belonging (Cohen, Steele, & Ross, 1999). Because faculty feedback can shape students' achievement narratives, it is worth considering the disconnect that can occur between a well-meaning professor who is judging work and the student who is trying to meet course expectations.

As an example, Helen historically offered very little feedback on assignments and tests, other than marking what students got wrong. She used question marks to indicate being unsure about what students were trying to communicate. In her mind, she was being helpful by pointing out students' mistakes or instances where they should clarify their responses. Through a request for detailed course feedback, Helen discovered that those students who earned low grades initially felt her grading indicated they were not cut out to learn organic chemistry. Her comments about the overall quality of work of the class, students said, reinforced that they did not belong there, at least not that semester. Many students focus on their grade on a specific assignment, determine whether they are satisfied with it (meaning they feel it is most likely justified and not worth getting clarification from professors), and then move onto the next assignment with little thought about what they did well or what they need to work on from the earlier assignment.

Nonetheless, what and how Helen chooses to communicate is important in shaping her students' growth mindset and belonging. As described in Chapter 1, students who were praised for their intelligence, a tactic reflecting a fixed mindset, were less likely to focus on learning and showed less task persistence than students who were praised for effort (Mueller & Dweck, 1998). Dweck (2014) purported that a single word—"yet"—can have a positive impact on students' views of learning and their roles in the process, as it reflects the growth mindset principle that learning is a process and that improvement requires focused effort and deliberate practice. Cohen and colleagues (1999) explored the impact on minority students of a message combining "an explicit invocation of high standards and an appropriate assurance that the student in question could meet such standards" (p. 1310). Because the messages increased students' task motivation and reduced their ratings of bias, the researchers labeled them "wise criticism" (p. 1310). See Table 3.1 for a list of questions and feedback to provide students that support growth mindset.

Table 3.1
Messages Supporting Growth Mindset

Questions to ask students	Feedback to give students
What did you learn from the homework or in-class activity?	I see you are working hard to master the material.
How do you feel when the coursework is challenging?	It is normal to struggle with this material, but trying new ways to learn it will help you break through.
What learning strategies are working for you?	Continue to refine how you approach your work and how much effort you put into learning.
How would you rate your effort on completing this work?	Keep working hard; effort is the key to learning challenging material.
What do you learn about yourself when you get an answer wrong?	You actually learn more by getting an answer wrong than by getting it right on the first try.
What did you learn from your performance on the quiz or test?	The areas that need improvement just mean you have not yet mastered them.

Helen could use these findings and recommendations to tailor her feedback on students' work. For example, when a student earned a low grade on an assignment, she could provide written or verbal feedback emphasizing that they had not yet mastered the concepts. Helen could also provide more detailed, wise criticism by reminding students of the high standards she is enforcing (e.g., telling students that organic chemists must be accurate in their formulas) and that she believes in their ability to rise to those standards.

To further encourage students to adopt growth mindset behaviors and enhance their sense of belonging, additional strategies to prompt them to read, reflect, and plan next steps in response to instructors' feedback include:

- giving students written feedback without the grade and requiring them to provide a summary of the feedback as their ticket to the grade,

- providing students with reflection questions (on the learning process and on overcoming obstacles) to answer before they can submit a revised draft or another assignment, and

- requiring students to submit a plan of action based on the feedback before they can submit a revised draft or another assignment.

Although these strategies take time to plan and implement, they are ways to get students to dig deeper into the process of receiving feedback and better understand what their next steps for improvement should be. These strategies are worth the investment of time by both parties because of the potential for improved outcomes. It is not enough to assume that students, especially those in the first year of college, know how to incorporate constructive criticism into future drafts or assignments.

Faculty can employ strategies to evaluate the effectiveness of growth-mindset and belonging interventions. For example, formative assessment, which can include quizzes, minute papers, or brief oral explanations, can help both students and faculty identify misconceptions or misapplications of information before high-stakes assignments. In fact, when used intentionally to emphasize growth mindset and belonging, formative assessment can reinforce these learning mindsets. The goal for faculty and students is to demonstrate on summative assessments, such as a final exam or major research paper, the improvement in understanding, application, or refinement of thought. Chapter 7 includes discussion of assessment of interventions and student outcomes in more detail.

Failure as Part of the Learning Process

The strategies outlined in this chapter assume that students are making the necessary improvements to raise their academic achievement and that, on some level, they make progress that is both measurable and desirable. However, what happens when a student who demonstrates growth mindset and belonging fails a course—or a semester's worth of courses? Or when a student does not earn a GPA high enough to get them into an academic program, keep their financial aid, or continue at the institution? A student who falls short of certain measures of achievement might feel as though their improvements were not enough. This experience could reinforce feelings of not belonging at the institution. The student might even decide they will never reach their goals.

Although it is impossible to ensure that all students achieve their goals within the time constraints of a semester or over the course of earning a degree, learning mindsets and belonging interventions can help students make incremental steps in improving their learning. Helen initially viewed her course as a way for students to reconsider their motivations and goals. A student who fails Helen's class—or any class—could use that experience as an opportunity to reevaluate their long-term goals and adjust them to align more clearly with their interests, values, and skills. Isn't that just part of the educational process, one might ask?

One way to consider such a question is to reason that failing within a course or failing an entire course itself can benefit the learning process—if the student views it within a growth mindset context. Even if students do not achieve as quickly as they or their institution hoped, there is still opportunity for progress, although it might mean adjusting their goals. Students who have suffered a setback significant enough to be placed on probation can also benefit from growth-mindset and belonging interventions. Stanford University's College Transition Collaborative, part of the Mindset Scholars Network, has created the Student Academic Standing Success Project, which aims to "reduce the stigma and shame felt by students who are placed on academic probation, increasing students' engagement with school resources and improving academic outcomes" (Mindset Scholars Network, 2015). Research by Waltenbury et al. (2018) focused on probation letters from a Canadian community college, in particular how an "attuned" probation letter's statements of growth mindset and belonging affect students' perceptions and actions while on probation. Waltenbury and colleagues found that when language around probation focuses on its temporary nature rather than making it a permanent label, students were more likely to have positive emotions and feel supported. Additionally, the research suggested that students on probation who received the attuned letter had higher GPAs the next semester than students who received the standard letter. Even when students experience multiple setbacks and failures, framing those experiences with growth mindset and belonging language has potential benefits.

Conclusion

Creating a classroom environment in which learning mindsets and belonging are part of the student's experience need not be a radical notion. However, certain disciplines, "killer courses," and faculty often serve as gatekeepers to further study or success for students. The argument that we must "weed out weak students" is fortunately fading in light of the research that has been cited in this chapter and the previous ones. For students to benefit from these strategies that increase belonging and harness the power of growth mindset, faculty must be willing to incorporate these concepts into their classes and communicate in ways that reinforce their principles.

Think back to Helen's story at the beginning of the chapter. If she truly wants to create a space in her classes for students to lean into the challenges that a course such as organic chemistry offers, then she will have to make concrete changes. Enrolling "better" students in her classes, as some faculty wistfully hope for, is not realistic nor necessary. Instead, Helen could work toward meeting her goals and those of the department with professional development that includes learning mindsets and strategies for creating inclusivity in the classroom. She could do this on her own or through a structured program or events at her institution. Then, she could identify the opportunities in her course when students could benefit the most from changes. One example: identifying a time in the semester in which crises of confidence might occur for students and helping them prepare for that unit with a scaffolded assignment, inclusion of everyday phrases, and opportunity for reflection. She will most likely need to continue this process of identifying areas of improvement, revision, and assessment of the effects of such changes.

Campus Conversations

The following questions are provided to begin conversations with key players on campus and as starting points for implementing change:

- In what ways can faculty incorporate learning mindsets, belonging, and resilience in their attitudes toward what and how they teach?

- What explicit and implicit messages do faculty give students about learning, challenges and setbacks, and belonging?

- In what ways can faculty revise written course materials to support growth mindset, belonging, and resilience?

- What everyday phrases can faculty use to reinforce growth mindset and belonging principles?

- Where are the crises of confidence in courses or degree programs, and how can faculty prepare students for them?

- How can faculty create meaningful feedback that supports growth mindset and is based on research on student achievement?

- What kinds of training and support do faculty need to create the intentional environments that support and enhance learning mindsets, belonging, and resilience?

Next Steps

The following steps are suggestions for moving from exploration to action:

1. Refer to Chapter 5 on campus culture as a starting point for discussing faculty's role in creating an atmosphere that supports learning mindsets, belonging, and resilience.

2. Assemble students, peer mentors, tutors, faculty, advisors, and administrators to talk about how the classroom environment can better support students who struggle with learning.

3. Discuss crisis-of-confidence points in degree plans. What can an institution do to better prepare students to overcome setbacks or feelings of inadequacy?

4. Work with the institution's director of professional development or teaching and learning center to establish a training program for faculty and other learning support specialists.

5. Find ways to recognize and reward faculty for improvements in their teaching as they relate to growth mindset, belonging, and resilience interventions.

References

Cohen, G. L., Steele, C. M., & Ross, L. D. (1999). The mentor's dilemma: Providing critical feedback across the racial divide. *Personality and Social Psychology Bulletin, 25*(10), 1302-1318. doi:10.1177/0146167299258011

Dweck, C. (2014). *The power of believing that you can improve.* Retrieved from https://www.ted.com/talks/carol_dweck_the_power_of_believing_that_you_can_improve

Fink, A., Cahill, M. J., McDaniel, M. A., Hoffman, A., & Frey, R. F. (2018). Improving general chemistry performance through a growth mindset intervention: Selective effects on underrepresented minorities. *Chemistry Education Research and Practice, 19*(3), 783.

Mindset Scholars Network. (2015). *Academic standing.* Retrieved April 22, 2019, from https://collegetransitioncollaborative.org/academic-standing/

Mueller, C. M., & Dweck, C. S. (1998). Praise for intelligence can undermine children's motivation and performance. *Journal of Personality and Social Psychology, 75*(1), 33-52. doi: 10.1037/0022-3514.75.1.33

Paunesku, D., Walton, G. M., Romero, C. L., Smith, E. N., Yeager, D. S., & Dweck, C. S. (2015). Mindset interventions are a scalable treatment for academic underachievement. *Psychological Science, 26*(6), 784-793.

Raudenbush, S. W. (1984). Magnitude of teacher expectancy effects on pupil IQ as a function of the credibility of expectancy induction: A synthesis of findings from 18 experiments. *Journal of Educational Psychology, 76,* 85-97. doi:10.1037/0022-0663.76.1.85

Rosenthal, R., & Jacobson, L. (1968). *Pygmalion in the classroom: Teacher expectation and pupils' intellectual development.* New York, NY: Holt, Rinehart & Winston.

Schmidt, J. J., Shumow, L., & Kackar-Cam, H. (2017). Does mindset intervention predict students' daily experience in classrooms? A comparison of seventh and ninth graders' trajectories. *Journal of Youth & Adolescence, 46*(3), 582-602.

Steele, C. M. (1992, April). Race and the schooling of Black Americans. *Atlantic Monthly, 69*(4), 68-78.

Steele, C. M. (1997). A threat in the air: How stereotypes shape the intellectual identities and performance of women and African Americans. *American Psychologist, 52,* 613-629.

Steele, C. M. (2010). *Whistling Vivaldi: How stereotypes affect us and what we can do.* New York, NY: Norton.

Waltenbury, M., Brady, S., Gallo, M., Redmond, N., Draper, S., & Fricker, T. (2018). *Academic probation: Evaluating the impact of academic standing notification letters on students.* Toronto, Ontario: Higher Education Quality Council of Ontario.

Walton, G. M., & Cohen, G. L. (2011). A brief social-belonging intervention improves academic and health outcomes of minority students. *Science, 331*(6023), 1447-1451. doi:10.1126/science.1198364

Yeager, D. (2014). *Creating and sustaining mindset change in developmental mathematics.* Carnegie Foundation for the Advancement of Teaching Keynote. Retrieved from https://mctcctl.files.wordpress.com/2014/09/david-yeager-keynote_mindset.pdf

Yeager, D. (2017, April 21). *Using mindsets to lift achievement: What I've learned so far.* Presentation at University of Notre Dame. Retrieved from https://vimeo.com/215063946

Yeager, D. S., & Dweck, C. S. (2012). Mindsets that promote resilience: When students believe that personal characteristics can be developed. *Educational Psychologist, 47*(4), 302-314.

Yeager, D. S., Walton, G. M., Brady, S. T., Akcinar, E. N., Paunesku, D., Keane, L., ... Gomez, E. M. (2016, June 14). Teaching a lay theory before college narrows achievement gaps at scale. *Proceedings of the National Academy of Sciences, 113*(24), E3341-E3348. http://doi.org/ggb7t2

Chapter 4

Mindset Interventions to Close the Achievement Gap

Doug Daugherty and Tim Steenbergh

Jasmin's Mindset Story: Finding Resilience

Jasmin grew up in middle-class, suburban Detroit. Her parents were educators and had graduated from one of the top state universities in the country. She had a 3.8 GPA in high school and was heavily recruited to play college softball. Jasmin was academically well prepared, driven, and had decided to go to graduate school before ever taking her first college course. I (Steenbergh) knew none of this when she walked into my office at the end of her first semester; I only knew that she was a first-year student who seemed a bit cold and distant.

Jasmin didn't warm up despite my efforts to connect around our shared connections to Detroit, where my father had grown up. I tried to hide my frustration over the fact that she had skipped the scheduling sessions offered to all of my advisees and was now asking me to assemble a workable schedule from the few courses that remained open. I did the best I could, sampling from several general education courses and adding a sophomore-level psychology course I thought she would enjoy.

This is the first interaction I remember having with Jasmin. At that time, I had no idea the challenges we would both face over the course of the next seven semesters. For her, those would involve finding her way as a Black student athlete on an all-White team at a predominantly White college. She would face questions about her hair, comments about her dress, and her teammates' negative views on the Black Lives Matter movement. For me, the challenges would mean learning about the difficulty of navigating our institution's White campus culture for students of color. And along the way, all of this would become more personal as my wife and I tried to help our newly adopted son navigate White culture.

We approach this chapter with some reluctance, as we are two middle-aged, White men with limited personal experience of prejudice. At times, we have found it hard to talk and write about the challenges some of our marginalized students face because their experiences are not our own. Although we do not share those experiences, we do share a common goal: their success. In our roles as practitioners, we have assumed responsibility for helping create a learning environment in which everyone can flourish, particularly students of color. We have been fortunate to learn from our students and others about some of the challenges they face, and we review those challenges here. We also discuss mindset interventions that have proven useful in closing the achievement gap. Finally, we describe some of the translational work we have done in this regard. We have implemented growth-mindset and social-belonging interventions pioneered by others in an effort to improve outcomes for first-generation students and students of color at our institution.

Segregation's Ongoing Reality

More than 60 years after the *Brown v. Board of Education* decision that declared segregation in U.S. schools unconstitutional, integration has still not been widely achieved. Today, most White students attend primary and secondary schools that are overwhelmingly White. Too many schools remain separate and unequal. In recent years, an increasingly divisive, fearful, and anti-other political climate has eroded integration gains (Cashin, 2014; Tatum, 2017). All this comes despite evidence demonstrating the benefits of integrated schools and communities. Those who live in integrated communities tend to be more open-minded and community-oriented, reporting greater satisfaction on average with neighborhoods than those who live in segregated communities (Cashin, 2014).

Although many factors have contributed to the failure to achieve school integration in the United States, several appear to be most central. These include implicit bias, negative stereotypes, prejudice, and discrimination; economic, political, and judicial inequalities; and a failure of a unified political will (sense of justice). A meaningful discussion of these factors goes well beyond the scope of this chapter and beyond the expertise of the authors. We have chosen to focus on several factors that are most pertinent to the observed achievement gap for students of color: implicit bias, discrimination, and stereotype threat. Awareness of these issues is vital to understanding the potential of mindset and other interventions in higher education.

Implicit Bias

Implicit bias involves unconscious, automatic responses rooted in assumptions about others; these are often based on race, ethnicity, or gender (Payne, Niemi, & Doris, 2018) and have been widely observed even among those who consciously reject racial stereotypes and actively support anti-discrimination efforts (Roberts, 2011). Rachel Godsil, director of research at the American Values Institute, noted:

> Implicit bias does not mean that people are hiding their racial prejudices. They literally do not know they have them. More than 85 percent of all Americans consider themselves to be unprejudiced. Yet researchers have concluded that

the majority of people in the United States hold some degree of implicit racial bias. (Roberts, 2011, para. 1)[1]

The bottom line is that humans tend to operate based on group stereotypes, particularly in response to those with whom we are less familiar because of divergent cultural backgrounds. Implicit bias needs to be well understood by those in higher education, particularly if we are to work effectively toward inclusion, equity, and justice for our students, faculty colleagues, and staff members.

The college years correspond with *emerging adulthood*, a developmental period of transition from adolescence to young adulthood (i.e., ages 18 to 29) that is marked by independent identity and role exploration (Arnett, 2000). This important period is also marked by the experience of institutionalized disadvantage for most adults of color (e.g., residential segregation, aggressive policing, employment inequalities, microaggressions; Hope, Hoggard, & Thomas, 2015).

In their review of the research on emerging adulthood and the impact of racism, Hope, Hoggard, and Thomas (2016) reiterated the role of discrimination in shaping the personal and sociopolitical development of emerging Black adults, citing increased risks and stress as well as the potential for maladaptive coping. Racial discrimination has been positively associated with the wear and tear of biological systems (i.e., allostatic load) at age 20, with indicators of biological stress widening during young and middle adulthood. Therefore, as Hope and colleagues (2016) assert:

> Any attempt to address the inequity faced by Black emerging adults should first deeply consider how this population's experiences with racial discrimination influence their psychological, physiological, and sociopolitical health—and how that makes an already challenging developmental period even more difficult. (p. 38)

The good news is that this stress load can be reduced by high levels of parental and peer support and by perceived favorable views of Blacks in the community (Brody et al., 2014; Geronimus, Hicken, Keene, & Bound, 2006).

Racial discrimination has also been associated with increased risks for mental health problems and psychological distress, such as depression, suicide, stress disorders, and substance abuse (Brown et al., 2000; Carter, 2007; Greene, Way, & Pahl, 2006; Polanco-Roman & Miranda, 2013; Sellers & Shelton, 2003). Remarkably, Black students who deemphasize race in an effort to fit in with the majority White campus community exhibit the strongest

---

[1]Interested readers are invited to visit Harvard University's Project Implicit at https://implicit.harvard.edu/implicit. The site offers a creative, empirical approach to self-assessment of implicit bias involving race, gender, sexual orientation, and other topics.

association between discrimination and depressive symptoms (Banks & Kohn-Wood, 2007). Again, we see the importance of a positive ethnic–racial–cultural identity, with racial identity as a major component of self. Pride in one's racial identity and group, rather than assimilation at all costs, appears to promote students' psychological well-being.

Historically, Blacks have been disempowered politically because of racism and discrimination. For emerging Black adults, then, sociopolitical and civic engagement can serve as an adaptive coping strategy, counteracting the stress associated with racial discrimination, reducing vulnerability, and promoting well-being (Hope & Spencer, in press). Civic engagement provides a means for Black students to work actively toward culture change, amending the socio-political conditions that contribute to their net vulnerability and stress (Hope et al., 2016).

This type of engagement ended up being an important aspect of Jasmin's undergraduate experience. She began to voice her concerns about the way she and other students of color were treated on campus. She wrestled with the decision to kneel during the national anthem at sporting events and discussed with the university's president and board members the need to make our institution more inclusive. Jasmin's response was one of resilience and, in time, she appeared to develop an understanding of just how much we needed her. Perhaps we should not have been surprised when, upon graduation, Jasmin turned down a full ride to another institution and chose to pursue graduate studies on our campus. She had found a purpose worth investing in.

Gabi's Identity Story: Reconnecting With Roots

Gabi was a quiet, unassuming Latina student. Prior to college, she lived in a small Midwest town with her mother and sister. Her high school was chronically underfunded and lacked a robust curriculum and strong teachers. Her community was almost entirely White, with few Hispanic residents. Gabi distanced herself from her father's Mexican heritage and native language, identifying instead with her mother, and tried to fit in with her peers and others in her community.

Psychologist Beverly Tatum (2017) suggested that Latinx adolescents such as Gabi commonly downplay their heritage in an effort to fit in with the majority culture of a predominately White, non-Hispanic school community. This process of assimilation can make it difficult to fully embrace a positive ethnic–cultural–racial identity that integrates the multiple dimensions of one's identity (i.e., intersectionality). These individuals, whether Black, Asian, Native American, or Latinx, male or female, often experience a developmental awakening as college students, with increased exposure to diverse peers, mentors, and allies as well as increased interest in reclaiming their diverse ethnoracial identities. The university environment often, although not always, provides psychological safety and support for navigating this process.

Gabi transitioned to our university without the benefit of a sizeable group of Latinx peers, faculty members, or staff. The campus culture was similar to her high school and, therefore, familiar to Gabi. She was an engaged, pleasing, and successful student who gradually connected with several peers and faculty members. Her sense of belonging was furthered by her religious beliefs, which were shared by many at the university. Despite these positive factors, however, Gabi's lingering doubts about belonging persisted as she continued to hide aspects of herself.

Gabi was reluctant to be transparent about her background and personal life until late in her junior year. As she identified more with her major and sense of calling, she became more open about her life. She started to connect with fellow students, faculty, and staff associated with her major. Some of her course readings, along with peers and faculty, explicitly and implicitly affirmed the belonging of diverse students. Psychologist Claude Steele referred to this phenomenon as development of classroom "niches, where the negative stereotypes about minority individuals don't apply" (qtd. in Tatum, 2017, p. 161). We have more to say about this later when we discuss stereotype threat.

Gabi started to share with others at the university more about her experiences as the daughter of a single mother and a geographically distant, Latino father. She shared her plans to see her father in Texas and to reconnect with her paternal grandparents as she expressed renewed interest in Spanish and her Mexican heritage. In doing so, she was becoming more fully known to herself and her university friends. During this time, I (Daugherty) recall sitting in on several office conversations between Gabi, other students, and Christy, our administrative assistant. Christy was a mother to many of our students, especially those such as Gabi who served as student assistants. As I observed or joined these conversations, I was struck by the apparent changes in Gabi. She seemed much more open, relaxed, and authentic.

Stereotype Threat

Steele tells a poignant story from his childhood, when he first awakened to the meaning of being Black in America (Steele, 2011). It was the beginning of summer break, and he was looking forward to swimming at the community pool through the summer. Then he learned that Black kids could not go to the pool except on Wednesday afternoons. This was his introduction to what he later called identity contingencies, environmental cues that suggest stereotypes may be pertinent and significant (Purdie-Vaughns, Steele, Davies, Ditlmann, & Crosby, 2008).

Over the course of Steele's remarkable career, he and his (former) graduate students have repeatedly demonstrated the profound effects of stereotypes and environmental cues on academic performance. Stereotype threat refers to underperformance, intellectual or otherwise, as a result of concerns about fulfilling a negative stereotype pertinent to one's identity (Steele, 2011). The effect of stereotype threat is subtle and easy to miss, yet profound.

More than 25 years of research overwhelmingly demonstrate that we are all subject to significant underperformance in the context of subtle cues reminding us of negative stereotypes involving our identities and the task at hand (Good, Aronson, & Inzlicht, 2003; Steele, 1992, 1997, 2003; Steele & Aronson, 1995). For example, students look to environmental cues, such as being asked to report race/ethnicity or gender just prior to a test of intelligence (e.g., math), to determine whether negative stereotypes might be pertinent in a particular context.

As a middle-aged White male (Daugherty), then, my performance is unencumbered by identity when the task involves intellectual performance or math—no negative stereotypes apply here. I am on much shakier ground, however, if the task involves dancing, athletic performance, or racial sensitivity, where negative stereotypes might apply, particularly if I really care about how I perform. Steele (2011) and colleagues have demonstrated the profound effect of stereotype threat on a wide variety of tasks (e.g., intelligence, achievement, and math tests; athletic performance; conversations about race) and identities (e.g., race/ethnicity; gender; age). He describes this as a "snake in the house" effect: If you know there is a snake in the house, it is hard not to be in a state of divided attention as you interact and move around. In other words, stereotype threat gets in your head, resulting in the underperformance that you fear most in that moment. Steenbergh and I recall one such experience all too vividly. We were at a national conference, addressing the topic of racial bias in the criminal justice system and our local findings regarding disparate Black–White referral rates for alternatives to incarceration. It happened that all the session attendees were Black. Although one of our co-presenters was Black, Steenbergh and I were very aware of our being White and the available stereotypes about racial insensitivity among Whites. It was a snake in the house (head) experience for Steenbergh and me: "Take care. Don't confirm the stereotype." But, sure enough, I blundered the first sentence out of my mouth, and Steenbergh did not fare much better.

Reducing the Impact of Stereotype Threat

Steele (2011) and Tatum (2017) offered several suggestions for reducing the negative impact of stereotype threat in higher education. In some cases, these remedies are simple and straightforward. In others, they are quite challenging and nuanced, requiring culture shifts in our classrooms and on our campuses. Three strategies that merit particular attention include:

- exposing students to diverse authors, sources, and role models of color;
- creating classrooms and subcultures (niches) where the negative stereotypes about various groups clearly do not apply; and

- communicating high expectations and confidence in students' capacity to achieve the standards (Dweck, Walton, & Cohen, 2014; Steele, 2003; Tatum, 2017).

Who Gets to Graduate?

Our own awakening to issues of belonging, disadvantage, and the intersectionality of identities was furthered by a *New York Times* article, "Who Gets to Graduate?" (Tough, 2014) in which the author noted that socioeconomic status (SES) is the best predictor of college graduation. Tough described the experience of Vanessa, a first-year student of color at the University of Texas (UT) at Austin. The daughter of a single mother whose hopes of college were dashed when she became pregnant, Vanessa and her relatives thought she would be the one to land the first college degree in their family. Unbeknownst to them, the odds were stacked against her. Tough wrote,

> To put it in blunt terms: Rich kids graduate; poor and working-class kids don't. Or, to put it more statistically: About a quarter of college freshmen born into the bottom half of the income distribution will manage to collect a bachelor's degree by age 24, while almost 90 percent of freshmen born into families in the top income quartile will go on to finish their degree. (p. 26)

Despite what many believe, aptitude, as measured by SAT scores, is a relatively weak predictor of college graduation relative to socioeconomic status (Estep, 2016). For example, consider students who score between 1000 and 1200 on the SAT. If these students come from families whose income is in the top 25% of the population, then 2 in 3 can expect to graduate from college. But low-income students in the bottom 25%, with similar SAT scores, demonstrate a 1 in 6 chance of persisting to graduation (Tough, 2014).

Tough (2014) explained that Vanessa struggled her first semester, doubting her abilities and her choice to attend UT Austin. She wrestled with questions such as "Am I supposed to be here?" and "Am I good enough?" Vanessa's story opened our eyes to the interaction of SES, educational disadvantage, mindset and belonging questions, and college adjustment. Educators talk about the achievement gap observed for college students of color, but we often fail to recognize the opportunity gap that precedes those differences. The opportunity gap involves disparities in school funding, resources, and quality that low-income students experience relative to middle- and higher-income families (Flores, 2007). These disparities, although more common for students of color, are certainly not unique to them.

J. D. Vance (2016) described his own experience with poverty and educational disadvantage as a first-generation White student in Appalachia. His story illustrates some of these disadvantages, from not knowing how to fill out financial aid forms or understanding Pell grants to trying to fit in with peers from very different backgrounds. Despite graduating college with honors, some of those socioeconomic challenges persisted into law school at Yale. Vance admitted, "I have never felt out of place in my entire life. But I did at Yale" (p. 202). He went on to explain that his lack of belonging stemmed from the fact that, despite diversity in other respects, more than 95% of Yale Law School students come from families with upper-middle class incomes or higher. In Vance's words, "Very few people at Yale Law School are like me. They may look like me, but for all the Ivy League's obsession with diversity, virtually everyone—Black, white, Jewish, Muslim, whatever—comes from intact families who never worry about money" (p. 203).

In *Place, Not Race: A New Vision of Opportunity in America*, Cashin (2014) argued that universities should pay a lot more attention to geographical and economic disadvantage than ethnicity or race. Like Vance, she noted that ethnoracial diversity without SES diversity is common for Ivy League schools. Cashin told the story of two students at Yale, one rural and White and the other Black and from the inner city. Because of similar backgrounds in terms of SES, the pair found they had far more in common with each other than race alone would suggest. Neither could relate to peers who always had money for eating out, movies, and other activities.

Mindset Interventions and Student Success

How do we help ensure the success of students whose racial or ethnic identities, social position, and economic challenges threaten their chances at a college degree? Tackling implicit biases and championing institutional culture change are noble solutions, but these represent complex initiatives that take vast amounts of time and resources. What can we offer students now that will help them successfully navigate the challenges of college and complete their degrees? The section that follows provides an overview of some mindset interventions that show promise. We offer these not as a way to sidestep broader institutional and cultural change, but as solutions that can work in conjunction with other institutional initiatives that promote the good of all students.

Growth-Mindset Interventions

Growth-mindset interventions aim to help students develop an incremental view of their intellectual abilities so they will persist in the face of challenges. As Chapters 1 and 2 describe, such interventions are intended to help students embrace challenges and focus on their growth as a result of believing they can get smarter. Credible evidence supports the effectiveness of these interventions. For example, a recent meta-analysis of 29 studies testing growth-mindset interventions against control groups found a small but significant effect (Sisk, Burgoyne, Sun, Butler, & Macnamara, 2018). However, when the researchers took into account the characteristics of who was receiving the intervention, the findings demonstrated that low-income students benefited most. Although growth-mindset interventions had little effect on middle-class and wealthier students, they produced a much bigger effect size ($d = .34$) for low-income students. For this group, such interventions appear to pay off in terms of better academic outcomes and, therefore, should be considered when addressing the achievement gaps described earlier in this chapter.

In some instances, growth-mindset interventions have been implemented indiscriminately and without sufficient forethought, resulting in little to no benefit. We prefer to focus on those that have produced benefits. Although some researchers might take us to task for "cherry picking," we believe the literature provides sufficient evidence for our claim that these interventions are most effective when they are true to the underlying theoretical foundations on which they were originally developed and when they are delivered to student groups where significant achievement gaps exist.

Aronson, Fried, and Good (2002) provided an example of a well-conceived growth-mindset intervention that specifically targeted Black college students. The researchers aimed to minimize the impact of stereotype threat and increase students' feelings of belonging by conveying that intelligence can grow with effort and persistence.

In this study, students in the experimental group learned about the malleability of intelligence. The intervention conveyed this by exposing the students to basic research findings and having them view a brief video clip. Each student was assigned as a pen pal to an at-risk, struggling middle school student. Each college participant received a letter (prepared by the researchers) from their pen pal, describing the difficulties they were experiencing in school. The participants first had to respond to the letter, encouraging the middle schoolers to continue to work hard and persist through their challenges. The college pen pals were asked to mention in their letters that research has shown that intelligence can grow "like a muscle." They were told that the goal was to show middle schoolers that college students were once like them and had to overcome challenges on their way to success. However, the unstated and actual objective of the exercise was to convince the letter writers of the malleability of their own intelligence, thereby minimizing the negative impact of stereotype threat that Black college students often experience.

The study design included a stealthy approach to mindset interventions (Robinson, 2010; Yeager & Walton, 2011). Rather than using a direct approach to address student mindsets—and potentially signaling that there was something wrong with them or the way they were thinking—this intervention took a more indirect approach.

The intervention had the desired effect. Letter writers, who had been indirectly taught about the malleability of intelligence, earned higher grades and reported enjoying and valuing school more than those from the two control groups. However, a particularly interesting result in this study, consistent with our earlier point about who benefits most from these interventions, was that Black students saw a greater benefit from the intervention relative to their White counterparts. In other words, Black students who wrote letters about the malleability of intelligence earned higher grades than their Black peers in the two control groups, while White students showed similar but less pronounced and persistent benefits.

The results of this study suggest the intervention had a powerful impact on students' learning mindsets. Consequently, as noted in Chapter 2, it is helpful to identify the particular features of the intervention that seemed to make a difference:

- It was based on an incremental theory of intelligence (Dweck, 2006), emphasizing that brains grow through effort.

- It actively involved students by engaging them in advocating for a growth mindset and conveying this message to what they believed was an authentic audience (sometimes called "saying is believing," first referenced in Chapter 2).

- It was delivered at a time when students might be vulnerable to negative perspectives relating to intelligence.

- Its stealthy delivery to both Black and White students, without mentioning that it was an "intervention," did not reinforce beliefs that the student was at risk or in need of help.

As a result, the intervention appeared to affect all students positively, with particular benefits for those considered at risk because of the negative effects of stereotype threat.

Social-Belonging Interventions

As Jasmin's and Gabi's stories remind us, when students feel like they don't belong or fit in, they often struggle to engage academically and fail to succeed. The past decade has seen increased efforts to deliver interventions that address students' sense of social belonging. Specifically, these interventions seek to normalize feelings of not fitting in and suggest meaningful connections will happen with time. Walton and Cohen (2011) conducted one of the most influential studies evaluating the effects of a social-belonging intervention. We describe it here to offer readers a better sense of what such a well-conceived intervention might entail.

Like the intervention just discussed, Walton and Cohen's (2011) effort was brief and simple. It aimed strategically to improve first-year students' sense of social belonging by framing social challenges as both normal and temporary. Participants were students in the second semester of their first year at a selective college. Those in the treatment group read what they were told was a research report detailing the results of a survey of senior students at their college. The report's findings indicated that most students initially worried about fitting in and finding their place but grew more comfortable and confident over time.

Next, students wrote an essay describing how their own experiences provided support for the findings of the survey. In the final step of the intervention, students were asked to convert their essay into a speech that could be shown to future first-year students to support them in their transition (speeches were recorded by a video camera). Students in the control group received a similar report, but its message focused on the changes in sociopolitical attitudes of senior students at their institution. Just like those in the treatment group, students in the control group had to develop an essay and deliver a speech. The intervention and the control experience lasted about an hour.

Results of their study paralleled those of Aronson and colleagues (2002), with the intervention having a pronounced impact on Black students. Whereas Black students in the control group showed no improvement in GPA, the outcome was different for those who received the social-belonging intervention. Black students whose essays and speeches focused on overcoming challenges related to social belonging earned GPAs that rose steadily from their first year through their senior year. In fact, their participation in the intervention put them on an upward trajectory that closed the GPA gap between them and their White peers by nearly 80%. These findings—demonstrated in a well-controlled, carefully conducted experiment—provide strong evidence of the recursive effects of well-designed learning-mindset interventions.

Readers might ask, What contributed to these positive gains in achievement? The researchers had the same question and, acting on a hunch informed by their research on social belonging, used daily surveys to examine the relationship between students' experiences with adversity and feelings of belonging. The results told a powerful story about the ways that challenges influence college students' (particularly those from underrepresented minority groups) perceptions of belonging. For students in the control group, perceptions of adversity were negatively correlated with feelings of belonging. This created an emotional roller coaster of sorts, with students' sense of belonging on campus rising and falling based on how easy or difficult the day had been. Things were different and more stable for students in the treatment group. In the words of Walton and Cohen (2011), "the intervention robbed adversity of its symbolic meaning for African-Americans, untethering their sense of belonging from daily hardship" (p. 1449). For this group, daily challenges no longer affected their sense of belonging. Further analysis revealed that this unleashing of social belongingness from experiences with adversity produced lasting changes, even three years after the intervention.

Again, we have tried to emphasize the most salient features of this intervention:

- It was grounded in psychological research on the relationship between social adversity and belonging.
- It targeted students' internal beliefs about social belonging and fitting in.
- It was delivered to students during their first year, leveraging the potential for learning mindsets to improve students' experience over time.

- It used a saying-is-believing strategy to help students personalize and internalize the message that struggling to fit in is a normal part of the college experience and is resolved over time.

Minding and Mending the Gap: Other Interventions With Marginalized Students

Growth mindset and belonging researchers highlighted several other psychosocial interventions in their review of empirically supported interventions and academic tenacity (Dweck et al., 2014; Yeager & Walton, 2011). For example, in a randomized control trial involving low- and middle-income Black middle school students, writing about values that students considered important boosted GPA by .30 for the term and by .46 over two years (Cohen, Garcia, Apfel, & Master, 2006; Cohen, Garcia, Purdie-Vaughns, Apfel, & Brzustoski, 2009).

Researchers found similar effects of values-affirmation interventions for female college students in a physics class. The intervention substantially reduced the gender gap relative to the control condition, both in terms of GPA and scores on a national exam (Miyake et al., 2010). Other interventions with research support have included efforts to make coursework personally relevant, communal rather than competitive, and consistent with positive racial and future selves (Yeager & Walton, 2011).

mSuccess: Delivering Mindset Interventions via Smartphone

Delivering mindset interventions for first-year students was not something we, the authors, had planned. As mentioned earlier, however, the *New York Times* article "Who Gets to Graduate?" alerted us to the national challenges facing higher education. Tough (2014) reported that fewer than half of U. S. college students in four-year and community colleges were graduating—the second-lowest graduation rate in the world, just above Hungary. We also had a growing awareness of how those realities were playing out on our own campus. A significant portion of our institution's students—especially first-generation and students of color—were not faring well. They arrived on our predominantly White, middle-class campus facing many of the challenges described earlier. And few of us felt well equipped to serve them.

Developing a Mobile Platform for Assessment and Intervention

Another important development took place in 2011 in our research lab that paved the way for our work. While searching for a way to better study people's daily experiences, we had landed on a technique that involves gathering data in the context of everyday life (Shiffman, Stone, & Hufford, 2008). Rather than using a survey to ask students about their experiences over the previous couple of weeks, or even over the course of the semester, we began using a smartphone app to find out what students were doing within the moments of their everyday lives.

In our initial study, first-year students loaded an app on their phones that sent them periodic notifications during their first semester. The app asked them questions such as, How many of the last 20 minutes have you spent on academics? and How many of the last 20 minutes have you wasted?, as well as other questions related to their experience (Runyan et al., 2013). In addition to learning more about how first-year students spent their time, we discovered that the experience had made an impact. At the end of the semester, we surveyed our app-carrying students, along with another group we had randomized not to carry the app, and asked how much time they had wasted that semester. Of students who carried the app, 80% reported that doing so made them more aware of how they had spent their time. They estimated wasting about 21% of their time that semester. Students in the control group, on the other hand, reported wasting 11% of their time.

Had the app caused our students to waste more time? That is one possible interpretation. The better one, supported by other data, was that the app made students more aware of how they spent their time. We concluded that the app was "training" students to pay better attention to how they used their time.

Our initial work with first-year students opened our eyes to the possibility and potential value of delivering mobile interventions to promote student success. That realization, and the aforementioned statistics on poor outcomes for students of color and first-generation students, pushed us forward. Around that time, Chris Devers, a friend of ours and a resident expert on learning, shared some of the growth mindset work of Dweck and the social-belonging work of Walton and Cohen. The positive outcomes they demonstrated and the sound theoretical grounding of their interventions persuaded us to consider how the students' mobile interaction could access the underlying psychological processes these learning theorists were targeting. We decided to deliver similar interventions to students' phones.

Intervention Context

To understand the context in which we delivered the mSuccess intervention, readers should know that we work at a religiously affiliated liberal arts college in rural, central Indiana. Our residential student body of roughly 3,000 historically has been predominantly White and middle or upper-middle class. However, in recent years, the college's administration has pursued greater diversity and has developed strategic initiatives focused on serving students of color. Recruiting efforts have yielded modest but significant gains in Black and Hispanic student enrollment. We also have continued to enroll significant numbers of first-generation students. Unfortunately, our retention rates for these students have not kept up with their enrollment numbers.

mSuccess Development and Delivery

In Fall 2015, we launched an initial pilot project to test the feasibility and potential impact of a mobile growth mindset and social-belonging intervention. We named the intervention mSuccess, borrowing from the field of medicine, where mobile health, or mHealth, has advanced rapidly. We delivered mSuccess to 72 first-year students enrolled in remedial math and English classes. Students were invited to download the app and interact with it during the first two weeks of the semester and again, briefly, around fall break. Students who downloaded the app would receive notifications. When they responded, the app would present content we had developed around growth mindset and social belonging, drawing on Walton and Cohen's (2007, 2011) work.

Results from the pilot study were encouraging. Engagement with the mSuccess intervention was clearly correlated with end-of-semester GPA ($r = .30$). And not surprisingly, given findings from other studies, we observed the correlation between app engagement and GPA as especially high among students of color ($r = .47$), suggesting that the more students engaged with the intervention, the better their first-semester GPA. Following these results, and with support from our administration, we launched an experimental study with our incoming first-year class the following year.

mSuccess 2.0

In summer 2016, we approached upper-level administrators in our student development office, asking to conduct an experimental study of mSuccess with all of our incoming first-year students. It was a bold request, but we made our case, backed with findings from our pilot study and copies of Walton and Cohen's (2011) work. Initial questions focused on what the interventions entailed and why we wanted to include all our students, rather than targeting only those deemed at risk. We explained that it was important to deliver the intervention in a somewhat stealthy way, so that students felt it was just a part of new-student orientation and not intentionally aimed at students of color or first-generation students. Questions about the use of a control group also surfaced after word got out that students of color had experienced particularly positive outcomes in our pilot. We explained the value of an experimental design in conclusively testing the effects of our intervention; we also referenced other institutions that used similar designs to test initiatives.

With the blessing of our student affairs office, we then shifted our attention to the logistics of separating students into intervention and control groups and engaging them as early as possible, so they could immediately benefit from the intervention. We hoped that by instilling adaptive learning mindsets at the outset of college, we could head off some of the social-belonging challenges common in the first few weeks of the first semester. We knew other institutions had delivered interventions in the summer as part of registration, but we believed delivering interventions when students were in the midst of doubts about belonging and when academic challenges began could provide additional value.

We chose to engage students during new-student orientation, which took place over a week to help incoming students acclimate to our institution before returning students arrived. We randomized students to either the mSuccess or control group. Students attended a 30-minute meeting in which they were asked to download "a mobile app designed to help you in the college adjustment process." Those in the intervention group then received three daily notifications for the first two weeks of the semester.

When the notifications came, students could swipe on their phone screens and, depending on which group they belonged to, receive either growth mindset and social-belonging prompts (intervention group) or general information about the university (control). The social-belonging interventions were delivered every other day—on Mondays, Wednesdays, and Fridays. Content included students' stories about how they struggled to fit in and how things worked out over time. Each story was accompanied by a picture, with each student's story and picture representing a variety of students (e.g., male, female, White, Black, Hispanic, Asian, first-generation). In addition to stories, students also were informed more generally about difficulties with belonging that most students experience. For example, a student might have received this information: "Almost all freshmen at Indiana Wesleyan and other schools worry about fitting in and being accepted by other students. So this is a common concern."

The growth-mindset intervention emphasized an incremental theory of intelligence and was delivered on Tuesdays, Thursdays, and Saturdays. As an example, one session included the statement, "When you learn new things, the cells and pathways in your brain multiply and improve. Effort and learning create new pathways in your brain and causes your brain cells to grow." That session was accompanied by an image of neural growth. On the next screen, students were told that "Some college assignments and tests can be pretty difficult. But, the more effort and time you spend learning, the more your intellectual skills and abilities grow. The result is a smarter and more capable you." Finally, students were asked, "How can you become smarter this week?" They provided a text response to that question and others, which were designed to help students more deeply consider, apply, and internalize the growth mindset messages being delivered.

mSuccess Results

Findings were consistent with what we had observed in the pilot. Receiving the mSuccess intervention showed a small but positive impact for all students, and it appeared to benefit students of color specifically. First-semester GPA of students of color receiving the mSuccess intervention averaged 3.41, whereas those in the control condition had an average GPA of 2.92. After one year, GPA differences persisted, suggesting this brief intervention had produced lasting effects. One-year retention rates were also significantly better for students of color who received the intervention, relative to those who did not (85% vs. 71%). Likewise, improved retention rates were observed for first-generation students who received mSuccess (78%) compared with those who did not (65%). Finally, as others have observed, among our White students, the intervention had little appreciable impact on GPA and retention rates.

Key Principles of the mSuccess Intervention

1. *Brevity.* We designed mobile interactions to take less than three minutes each, and most lasted less than one minute. Further, we only delivered the interventions during the first two weeks of the semester rather than extending it throughout the semester, as studies of many mindset interventions show that duration is unrelated to success rate (Sisk et al., 2018). In our pilot intervention, we found that few students engaged with a mid-semester booster session, so we dropped it from our later intervention. This fit more generally with our understanding that the mechanism of action in mindset interventions involves their recursive effects (Yeager, Walton, & Cohen, 2013). In other words, once a mindset is presented and begins to take hold, the student will interpret future experiences in light of that mindset, which serves to reinforce and strengthen it.

2. *Stealthy delivery.* One of the challenges in delivering mindset interventions is engaging students without signaling that they are being targeted specifically. We are especially mindful of this when working with marginalized groups, for whom negative stereotype threat can easily be triggered. Therefore, we framed the intervention in terms of an app designed to help all students transition during their first few weeks.

3. *Saying is believing.* The growth-mindset and social-belonging interventions highlighted earlier in the chapter required students to take their respective messages and repackage them in their own words to benefit others. To some extent, we also tried to incorporate a saying-is-believing strategy by programming the app to ask students to take the information we were sharing on belonging and growth mindset and put it into their own words, for others' benefit. Others have used this approach successfully to deliver growth-mindset and social-belonging interventions (e.g., Aronson et al., 2002; Walton & Cohen, 2011), and it is rooted in social psychology research (Higgins & Rholes, 1978).

4. *Ease of use.* Mobile interventions, in particular, should be easy to use, as students are used to interacting with well-designed, intuitive smartphone apps. User frustration, resulting from confusing app design or poor functioning, can quickly turn off those who tend to delete apps they do not like. After students downloaded our intervention app, it largely ran on its own, sending daily notifications

reminding students to engage the content and offering a simple user interface that allowed them to move seamlessly from notifications to content and then navigate easily through the intervention.

Lessons Learned from mSuccess

Several lessons surfaced as we designed, delivered, and evaluated the mSuccess intervention. Below are some key takeaways we hope might benefit others looking to deliver mindset interventions to their students.

1. *Campus collaboration is key.* One aspect that surprised us, initially, was the amount of coordination required with other institutional offices. Two of our key partners were our vice president for student development and the new-student orientation (NSO) committee chair. Both individuals helped us understand the structure of new-student initiatives and the layout of NSO. Since our initial delivery of mSuccess, we continue to appreciate the support of our Student Development Office and NSO committee in making mSuccess better.

2. *Personal engagement.* One way we have improved the mSuccess intervention since its inception is by moving student engagement to the first-year course. Large-scale, largely impersonal requests, both by email and in person, produced lower than expected engagement rates. With the NSO's help, we recruited peer educators from each of our institution's first-year courses to assist us with ensuring students downloaded the intervention during NSO week. This improved our engagement rates from about 50% to more than 75%. However, the past year saw a dip in engagement, something we blame on poor coordination on our end. Despite all the technological tools available, we might need to focus more on high-touch enrollment practices to maximize reach and impact of mSuccess.

3. *Murphy's law applies.* Having several hundred students interact with our system simultaneously when we first launched mSuccess was not something we thought through. In our case, the biggest challenges involved the amount of data our server would have to handle while hundreds of students downloaded the app, created an account, and responded to initial questions. All of this required Wi-Fi coverage and bandwidth, and we did not sufficiently estimate the demands this would place on our server. Lesson learned: Those using a server should ensure they are ready on launch with the university's president and board members to avoid delays and student frustrations, which can result in less engagement with the intervention.

4. ***A little mindset intervention goes a long way.*** We had read about the recursive effects of mindset interventions, and we were especially impressed with the four-year outcomes Walton and Cohen (2011) reported from their one-hour social-belonging intervention. But we had no idea how much exposure was enough to produce a difference. When we looked at the actual level of engagement with mSuccess, we found that, on average, students responded only to seven notifications (although students of color responded more frequently). Although we don't have the exact amount of time they spent in each session, we estimate that it was under 20 minutes. A modest intervention can have a big impact, and we believe that too large an intervention might even have paradoxical effects. Recall our earlier comments about the merits of a stealthy approach.

Conclusion

When explaining the causes of an individual's behavior, personality psychologists often reference the person–situation interaction. This framework is helpful for better understanding and addressing the challenges many students in higher education face. Implicit bias and other forms of discrimination contribute to the difficulties that many marginalized students experience and, no doubt, help shape these students' mindsets. In this chapter, we have offered what we think is a useful way forward in promoting healthy academic mindsets, also recognizing that greater institutional and cultural change are desperately needed. On a personal front, I (Steenbergh) am reminded of the challenges my wife and I have faced on this front since introducing our adopted son into our predominantly White rural community. We are responsible for promoting greater awareness and inclusion in our school system, our church, and our community while helping our son navigate the implicit (and sometimes explicit) biases and discrimination that exist.

Campus Conversations

The following questions are provided to begin conversations with key players on campus and as starting points for implementing change:

- What achievement gaps on our campus are better understood as opportunity gaps?
- Where on campus are students encouraged to identify with a group identity that may trigger negative stereotype bias?
- To what extent does our admissions team consider geographic and economic factors in promoting a diverse student body?

- What are some of the stories our marginalized students tell about struggling to connect on our campus, and how can we learn from their experiences?

Next Steps

The following steps are suggestions for moving from exploration to action:

1. Explore your implicit biases by taking a test on the Project Implicit website (https://implicit.harvard.edu/implicit/) and then discuss your findings with a colleague. Or consider taking it with colleagues and discussing your findings together.

2. Connect with a student who comes from a marginalized group on your campus and ask them if they will meet periodically over lunch (your treat) to talk about their experiences and the ways your institution can more effectively create an inclusive learning environment.

3. Identify an achievement gap on your campus and develop a strategy to address it. It may be helpful to start simple—perhaps with a class or a department that is willing—and then iterate over time, as you learn more about the opportunity gaps and psychological processes that perpetuate the problem.

References

Arnett, J. J. (2000). Emerging adulthood: A theory of development from the late teens through the twenties. *American Psychologist, 55,* 469-480.

Aronson, J., Fried, C., & Good, C. (2002). Reducing the effects of stereotype threat on African American college students by shaping theories of intelligence. *Journal of Experimental Social Psychology, 38,* 113-125.

Banks, K. H., & Kohn-Wood, L. P. (2007). The influence of racial identity profiles on the relationship between racial discrimination and depressive symptoms. *Journal of Black Psychology, 33,* 331-354.

Brody, G. H., Lei, M. K., Chae, D. H., Yu, T., Kogan, S. M., & Beach, S. R. (2014). Perceived discrimination among African American adolescents and allostatic load: A longitudinal analysis with buffering effects. *Child Development, 85,* 989-1002. http://doi.org/ggd6t8

Brown, T. N., Williams, D. R., Jackson, J. S., Neighbors, H. W., Torres, M., Sellers, S. L., & Brown, K. T. (2000). "Being black and feeling blue": The mental health consequences of racial discrimination. *Race and Society, 2,* 117-131. http://doi.org/fjvgpf

Carter, R. T. (2007). Racism and psychological and emotional injury recognizing and assessing race-based traumatic stress. *Counseling Psychologist, 35,* 13-105. http://doi.org/ftkw2v

Cashin, S. (2014). *Place, not race: A new vision of opportunity in America.* Boston, MA: Beacon Press.

Cohen, G. L., Garcia, J., Apfel, N., & Master, A. (2006). Reducing the racial achievement gap: A social–psychological intervention. *Science, 313,* 1307-1310.

Cohen, G. L., Garcia, J., Purdie-Vaughns, V., Apfel, N., & Brzustoski, P. (2009). Recursive processes in self-affirmation: Intervening to close the minority achievement gap. *Science, 324,* 400-403.

Dweck, C. S. (2006). *Mindset: The new psychology of success.* New York, NY: Random House.

Dweck, C. S., Walton, G. M., & Cohen, G. L. (2014). *Academic tenacity: Mindsets and skills that promote long-term learning.* Seattle, WA: Bill and Melinda Gates Foundation.

Estep, T. M. (2016). *The graduation gap and socioeconomic status: Using stereotype threat to explain graduation rates.* American Psychological Association. Retrieved from http://www.apa.org/pi/ses/resources/indicator/2016/10/graduation-gap.aspx

Flores, A. (2007). Examining disparities in mathematics education: Achievement gap or opportunity gap? *The High School Journal, 91,* 29-42.

Geronimus, A. T., Hicken, M., Keene, D., & Bound, J. (2006). "Weathering" and age patterns of allostatic load scores among blacks and whites in the United States. *American Journal of Public Health, 96,* 826-833. http://doi.org/dr55vz

Good, C., Aronson, J. M., & Inzlicht, M. (2003). Improving adolescents' standardized test performance: An intervention to reduce the effects of stereotype threat. *Journal of Applied Developmental Psychology, 24*(6): 645-662.

Greene, M. L., Way, N., & Pahl, K. (2006). Trajectories of perceived adult and peer discrimination among Black, Latino, and Asian American adolescents: Patterns and psychological correlates. *Developmental Psychology, 42,* 218-236.

Higgins, E. T., & Rholes, W. S. (1978). "Saying is believing": Effects of message modification on memory and liking for the person described. *Journal of Experimental Social Psychology, 14,* 363-378.

Hope, E. C., Hoggard, L. S., & Thomas, A. (2015). Emerging into adulthood in the face of racial discrimination: Physiological, psychological, and sociopolitical consequences for African American youth. *Translational Issues in Psychological Science, 1*(4), 342-351.

Hope, E. C., Hoggard, L. S., & Thomas, A. (2016, June). CE corner: Becoming an adult in the face of racism. *Monitor on Psychology, 47*(6), 35-38.

Hope, E., & Spencer, M. B. (in press). Civic engagement as an adaptive coping response to conditions of inequality: An application of phenomenological variant of ecological systems theory (PVEST). In N. Cabrera & B. Leyendecker (Eds.), *Handbook of positive development of minority children.* Dordrecht, Netherlands: Springer.

Miyake, A., Kost-Smith, L. A., Finkelstein, N. D., Pollock, S. J., Cohen, G. L., & Ito, T. A. (2010). Reducing the gender achievement gap in college science: A classroom study of values affirmation. *Science, 330,* 1234-1237.

Payne, K., Niemi, L., & Doris, J. M. (2018, March 27). How to think about "implicit bias." *Scientific American*. Retrieved from https://www.scientificamerican.com/article/how-to-think-about-implicit-bias/

Polanco-Roman, L., & Miranda, R. (2013). Culturally related stress, hopelessness, and vulnerability to depressive symptoms and suicidal ideation in emerging adulthood. *Behavior Therapy, 44*(1), 75-87. http://doi.org/bs22

Purdie-Vaughns, V., Steele, C. M., Davies, P. G., Ditlmann, R., & Crosby, J. R. (2008). Social identity contingencies: How diversity cues signal threat or safety for African Americans in mainstream institutions. *Journal of Personality and Social Psychology, 94*, 615-630.

Roberts, H. (2011). Implicit bias and social justice. *Open Society Foundations*. Retrieved from https://www.opensocietyfoundations.org/voices/implicit-bias-and-social-justice

Robinson, T. N. (2010). Stealth interventions for obesity prevention and control: Motivating behavioral change. In L. Dube, A. Bechara, A. Dagher, A. Drewnowski, J. Lebel, P. James, & R. Y. Yada (Eds.), *Obesity prevention: The role of brain and society on individual behavior* (pp. 319-327). London, England: Academic Press.

Runyan, J. D., Steenbergh, T. A., Bainbridge, C., Daugherty, D. A., Oke, L., & Fry, B. N. (2013). A smartphone ecological momentary assessment/intervention "app" for collecting real-time data and promoting self-awareness. *PLoS ONE, 8*(8), 1-9.

Sellers, R. M., & Shelton, J. N. (2003). The role of racial identity in perceived racial discrimination. *Journal of Personality and Social Psychology, 84*, 1079-1092. http://doi.org/db45hc

Shiffman, S., Stone, A. S., & Hufford, M. R. (2008). Ecological momentary assessment. *Annual Review of Clinical Psychology, 4*, 1-32.

Sisk, V. F., Burgoyne, A. P., Sun, J., Butler, J. L., & Macnamara, B. N. (2018). To what extent and under which circumstances are growth mind-sets important to academic achievement? Two meta-analyses. *Psychological Science, 29*(4), 549-571.

Steele, C. (1992). Race and the schooling of Black Americans. *Atlantic, 269*(4), 68-78.

Steele, C. (1997). A threat in the air: How stereotypes shape intellectual identity and performance. *American Psychologist, 52*(6): 613-629.

Steele, C. (2003). Stereotype threat and African-American student achievement. In T. Perry, C. Steele, & A. Hilliard, III (Eds.), *Young, gifted, and Black: Promoting high achievement among African-American students* (pp.109-130). Boston, MA: Beacon Press.

Steele, C. M. (2011). *Whistling Vivaldi: How stereotypes affect us and what we can do.* New York, NY: Norton.

Steele, C., & Aronson, J. (1995). Stereotype threat and the intellectual test performance of African Americans. *Journal of Personality and Social Psychology, 69*(5): 797-811.

Tatum, B. D. (2017). *Why are all of the Black kids sitting together in the cafeteria? And other conversations about race.* New York, NY: Basic Books.

Tough, P. (2014, May 15). Who gets to graduate? *The New York Times Magazine, 18,* 26-30.

Vance, J. D. (2016). *Hillbilly elegy: A memoir of a family and culture in crisis.* New York, NY: Harper.

Walton, G. M., & Cohen, G. L. (2007). A question of belonging: Race, social fit, and achievement. *Journal of Personality and Social Psychology, 92*(1), 82-96.

Walton, G. M., & Cohen, G. L. (2011). A brief social-belonging intervention improves academic and health outcomes for minority students. *Science, 331,* 1447-1451.

Yeager, D. S., & Walton, G. M. (2011). Social–psychological interventions in education: They're not magic. *Review of Educational Research, 81,* 267-301.

Yeager, D., Walton, G., & Cohen, G. L. (2013). Addressing achievement gaps with psychological interventions. *Kappan, 95,* 62-65.

Chapter 5

Changing Campus Culture to Foster Learning Mindsets

Latoya Lewis

Daniel's Learning Mindset Story: Thriving Among Contradictions

Daniel, along with six other students, had the opportunity to share a grit story, originally written as a class assignment, in front of 100 attendees at a campuswide summit on the subject. Each student's story revealed how they struggled with belonging, mindset, and resilience at some point in their lives.

In the opening lines of his story, Daniel talked about the contradiction of life: Sometimes "she" (life) can be great, but at other times, "she throws you down on the ground." Daniel then posed a question that expressed his truth—how he once felt about his own life: "What do you do when you are born already on the ground, being stomped on?"

As a Hispanic American, first-generation college student raised by a single parent living in poverty, school for Daniel was not a place for learning; rather, it was an opportunity to get a free meal. Like many impoverished students, Daniel's school breakfast and lunch might have been his only meals for the day, so he relied on school to meet this basic need. Although it fed him, school did not satisfy his need for acceptance. Because his fellow classmates experienced a similar level of poverty, they could not pick on one another because of what some had and others did not. They could identify one another's differences, however, and these differences became the root of the bullying Daniel experienced.

Feeling as if he did not belong in school and trying to protect himself from those who bullied him because of his ethnicity, Daniel created a shell. Inside his shell, he was free from the harassment. He isolated himself from classmates and refused help from others, including his teachers. Even at home, he perpetuated this protective device. Because his family was the cause of his many struggles, he did not feel they could help him. Living this way created a fixed mindset in Daniel. He was who he was, based on how others in his world viewed him: poor, Hispanic, a bastard.

When Daniel entered high school, his new environment provided more than a space for learning. It also meant new possibilities. New students and circumstances gave him a renewed outlook. Daniel no longer needed to be in his shell. He took a chance at belonging by joining the high school football team, and it worked. He had a community and more confidence. He developed a desire to prove wrong those people who told his mother he would never amount to anything. In fact, this feeling became stronger than his desire to remain inside his shell. Emboldened, he opened up, and the student who previously had done "just OK" in school graduated high school and began life as a community college student.

Once a student who did not have a single positive educational experience to draw from, Daniel now aspires to be a math teacher and is pursuing a degree in education. He hopes his future students will not have the same kinds of educational experiences he did. As a teacher, Daniel wants to let students from similar backgrounds know there is someone with whom they can identify. He wants to be the support system that he did not have—either because it did not exist or because he was so deep in his shell that he did not recognize it.

As Daniel told his story at the campuswide summit, there were few dry eyes in the audience. A moment of relief filled the room as the story shifted from defeat to hope, when Daniel described changing his perspective on life and himself. When he achieves his dream of teaching, Daniel wants to be *that* teacher—the one his students relate to. Although this is admirable and necessary, being one person, one teacher is not enough.

The beginning of Daniel's story is heartbreaking. Unfortunately, Daniel is not the only author of such a tale. For many other students, especially those from low-income households, school is a negative experience. For those struggling as Daniel did, school does not enrich their lives; it becomes yet another place that echoes or reinforces the negative messages and beliefs the students have of themselves. School did not provide the type of support Daniel needed in his formative years. Indeed, his school's culture did not support growth mindset, belonging, and resilience. Because of Daniel's culture—his brown skin, native Spanish language, and the many practices and customs shared by those of his ethnicity—he was set apart, labeled, and bullied. School could have been another culture with which Daniel identified, but he did not. Because he did not see the beliefs, values, and practices of school as inclusive, he created a shell to survive.

On a Mission

Creating or revamping a culture requires work on multiple levels. Before the work can start, however, an institution must ask, What are we working toward? A mission statement provides focus for the work of an institution, and when written effectively, it can be a tool or gauge by which to assess the work being done. The mission statement should be the foundation for everything the institution does. As such, all activities, behaviors, and goals should be driven by, and point back to, the mission. The mission statement should also help faculty, staff, administrators, and students understand their purpose and why they belong at the institution.

Even though such a statement might have existed long before the current faculty, staff, and students ever set foot on the campus, and even if only the institution's leaders are involved in rewriting it, all parties can make sure the beliefs behind the statement are put into action. The statement can bring a campus together around shared beliefs, draw students and employees to an institution, and be the reason a student develops an affinity to the college.

Many higher education mission statements can be summarized as:

> Our mission is to help students achieve excellence through the degree programs we offer so that they will be equipped to make the world a better place.

Such a mission may be inspirational, but its lofty ideal provides little insight into how the institution defines excellence or will help students achieve excellence. Additionally, this statement does not reflect the culture of learning mindsets. To revise a mission statement or create a new one that privileges belonging, resilience, and growth mindset, stakeholders might begin by answering the following questions:

- Why are these concepts important?
- What do we believe to be true about these concepts?
- How can we support these concepts?
- What are we currently doing that signals the value of these concepts to students, faculty, and staff?
- What might we be doing that sends an unintended or counterproductive message to members of our community about these concepts?

Answering these questions might lead to a revised mission statement, similar to the following:

> Our mission is to help students persist in light of the challenges they face in pursuit of excellence. We will provide degree programs and nonacademic experiences that meet the needs and interests of our students. When students leave our institution, they will be equipped with skills and resources to make the world a better place.

This statement addresses belonging (i.e., providing nonacademic experiences that meet students' needs and interests), resilience (i.e., helping students persist in light of challenges), and growth mindset (i.e., equipping them with skills and resources).

The mission statement, then, expresses an institution's beliefs and serves as a promise made to every student. A clear statement allows students to develop expectations for the experiences they will have at an institution. Should they expect only to earn a degree? Or can they expect to receive the support they may need to earn that degree? The institutional mission statement may be further operationalized at the unit or course level.

College-Wide Mission Statements

Faculty and staff can have a hand in writing or revising the mission statements for their individual departments. For example, staff in student services or academic support can help craft a statement that focuses on building resilience so that more students persist. Student life can ensure that its statement focuses on students' sense of belonging, and the mission statement for student affairs can state how the department will help students develop a growth mindset through courses they take.

Departmental mission statements guide the work of faculty and staff with their students, but sharing mission statements with students may also have a powerful impact. Research by Yeager and Walton (2011) suggests that exposing students to messages about belonging can be beneficial, especially when students have the opportunity to reflect on those messages and reinterpret them through writing about their own experiences. When students have opportunities to reflect on departmental mission statements, they can begin to identify with the smaller organizational unit within the college or university and hopefully begin to feel as if they belong there.

Mission Statements in the Classroom

Introduction to Teaching, a common course in teacher education programs in the United States, explores pedagogy, the history of American education, educational philosophies, and legal issues in the field. Students also begin to analyze issues connected to equity and the culture of K-12 classrooms. One assignment tied to this last outcome involves student teachers creating their own classroom culture for their future classes. The student teachers apply what they are learning to establish expectations, rewards, consequences, and even seating arrangements that encourage learning and limit distractions to the learning process. In creating a classroom culture, future teachers attempt to create environments that are more than mere spaces for learning. The aim is to make students feel safe and *empowered* to learn.

Another component of the classroom culture assignment requires student teachers to create a mission statement that promotes their ideal class environment. In three to five sentences, this statement establishes and expresses a set of classroom beliefs and goals that become the foundation for the dynamic between teacher and student. Here are sample mission statements written by students in the Introduction to Teaching course:

- "In our classroom, we will be responsible for our work and try our hardest to be the best that we can be. We will be respectful toward our fellow classmates and others. We will follow our classroom rules to succeed."

- "We, the stunning fifth-grade class, are here to learn, work together, and have an enjoyable time by being courteous, respectful, and maintaining positive minds to expand our knowledge and show people what we are capable of."

- "Our mission is to build each other up and not put each other down. We will encourage each other to do our best, be respectful, and work hard every day to be the best that we can be."

Each of these statements is inclusive, aiming to create a community of learners who are all in the experience together.

Mission statements are not exclusive to K-12 classrooms. They can also be written for college courses. The following mission statements might appear on syllabi for introductory English and math courses, respectively.

- In this class, we will approach writing as a process, and in following this process, we will grow in our ability to write academically and think about our writing. We will engage in this process both individually and collaboratively in order to produce academic essays.

- We will work to lessen any negative feelings we may have about math by learning processes and solving problems together. We will do practice assignments, ask questions of our teacher and peers, and attend tutoring until the math makes sense.

Instructors might also consider inviting their students into the mission statement writing process. In doing so, they can create a stronger classroom community where all voices are heard and validated and where everyone understands what is expected and is working toward a common goal.

The mission statement allows students to commit to who they will be for the upcoming year and, perhaps, to the people they will become in the future. In this community, if a student gets off track, their classroom's mission statement can serve as a reminder, and because others also are working according to the statement, there is built-in accountability. Additionally, when posted on a classroom wall, included on the landing page of the course website, or written on exams, the mission statement is a constant reminder that students are a part of a larger community. Reading the mission statement can encourage students to persist when they encounter challenges.

Evidence of the Culture

A mission statement, although important, is only the first step in establishing a culture at an institution that fosters growth mindset, belonging, and resilience. Evidence of such a culture can and should exist beyond the classroom. It should be apparent in the people, messaging, and programs that promote the beliefs of the institution.

Recruiting the Right People: Faculty and Staff

Learning mindsets are not just a subject educators should aspire to instill in students. To truly support students in these areas, it is important that those who work for the institution actively support the college's mission.

Faculty and staff are vital to an inclusive and resilient campus culture. Whom an institution hires and how it develops them is key to bringing the culture to life. An institution's mission might be the reason prospective faculty and staff apply, but the interview is an opportunity to find out how invested a candidate is in the areas of belonging, resilience, and growth mindset. Does an institution want applicants who are merely a good fit for a position or people who can embrace and grow the institutional culture? Table 5.1 features prompts that interviewers can use to help identify growth mindset, resilience, and belonging in potential employees.

An institution should weigh each of these concepts and their level of importance for a particular position and whether attitudes, values, and behaviors associated with learning mindsets need to be present when faculty and staff join the institution or whether these

Table 5.1

Interview Prompts to Ask Prospective Faculty and Staff

On belonging	On resilience	On growth mindset
What can you do/have you done in previous roles to ensure that students, colleagues, or customers feel that they are a part of what you are doing?	Talk about a time when you accomplished a goal despite being in the middle of a difficult circumstance.	What type of student will be successful in college courses?
When have you felt that you really belonged? Conversely, share about a time when you felt like you did not belong.	What is a major challenge you have faced, and how did you handle it?	Talk about a time when you had to change your way of thinking to accomplish a task.
It is common for students to feel a bit isolated when they begin college or when they start a new job. How important is helping people develop a sense of belonging? What are some things that help promote that?		How might you respond to a student who seems unprepared for the academic challenges of your class? How do you think about this student?
		Give an example of growth mindset in your own life.
		Talk about some new things you have learned lately.

characteristics can be cultivated through professional development initiatives. For example, how important is a strong sense of belonging for a candidate, and to what degree can the institution support belonging through professional development? Is it more important that someone joining the institution has a growth mindset or shows resilience, or is the institution willing to hire someone who is open to these ideas but may need help developing in these areas? Answers to these questions might vary by department and even role.

Recruiting the Right People: Students

Although colleges and universities may recruit high-achieving students from a range of social and economic backgrounds, they seem to have a propensity to recruit from schools where students do not face as many disadvantages (Jaschik, 2018a). Recruiting activities frequently focus on students who attend well-resourced public and private high schools and whose families have higher incomes. Many of these schools also have predominantly White student bodies. To include more low-income and underrepresented groups in their recruiting classes, colleges and universities will need to cast a wider net. Doing so also sends the message that institutions want traditionally underrepresented students on their campuses.

Some tactics for recruiting a diverse pool of student applicants include providing travel expenses to bring students from underrepresented groups to campus and sending staff to under-resourced areas to help prospective students complete financial aid paperwork. Other steps include marketing in languages other than English and offering free tuition to low- to moderate-income students (Goldstein, 2017). Colleges and universities can also send admissions representatives to low-income and racially diverse high schools.

The application process. During the admissions process, an institution will rely on students' test scores and personal statements, but it should also look for students who may be capable of succeeding despite lower grades or test scores and who may benefit from an environment where they can develop learning mindsets and belonging. In fact, many colleges and universities have adopted a more holistic review of applicants, moving away from solely using test scores and grades to determine which students should be admitted.

Although moving to this practice may be seen as "watering down" the admissions criteria, some institutions, such as Louisiana State University (LSU), have found success in taking a more holistic approach to reviewing applications. Under a new policy, the university exempted up to 4% of its applicants from the traditional admissions requirements: a 3.5 GPA or a minimum score of 25 on the ACT. Instead, the college looked closely at high school transcripts to evaluate course rigor, grade trends, and the types of courses students took in high school. Such an approach helped the university identify students who "show promise and potential for college success" (Jaschik, 2018b, para. 4). The first-year class size increased, while maintaining a mean GPA of 3.5 and a mean ACT score of 26 (i.e., one point higher than the minimum required score). Additionally, the number of admitted minority students increased even though race and ethnicity were not a part of the holistic admissions review. These gains speak to the power of holistic admissions. Vice President for Enrollment Management Jose Aviles said, "Students can see themselves at LSU, and not simply a cutoff score where certain groups of students might self-select to not even apply" (Jaschik, 2018a).

Another way to encourage a more holistic admissions process is to place greater emphasis on college essays and interviews, especially for students who may not rank at the top of the candidate pool in terms of high school grades and test scores. This strategy also provides students an opportunity to describe their mindsets and offer evidence of resilience. Knowing students from this perspective allows the institution to identify interventions that will best help them when they arrive on campus, after the first exam, or even at the end of the first semester.

The application essay. Nearly every college application asks students to write an essay. In keeping with this strategy, the institution can create essay prompts that are a tool to share its expectations for students or that are a window into the school's mission and values. The essay can tap into a student's understanding of growth mindset, resilience, and belonging and how these ideas are connected to being a part of an institution of higher learning, or it can ask students to reflect on their experience demonstrating such characteristics. The essay response will allow the admissions committee to see the extent to which students demonstrate learning mindsets and to assess the likelihood that the students will benefit from, and make positive contributions to, the culture that is defined by learning mindsets. The following are sample prompts that institutions can use:

- Describe a time when you faced and overcame a significant obstacle in your life.

- Recount a time when you faced a challenge, setback, or failure. How did it affect you, and what did you learn from the experience?

- Describe a problem you have solved or would like to solve. It can be an intellectual challenge, a research query, an ethical dilemma, or anything of personal importance, no matter the scale. Explain its significance to you and the steps you took (or might take) to identify a solution.

- Discuss an accomplishment, event, or realization that sparked a period of personal growth and a new understanding of yourself or others.

- Describe a topic, idea, or concept you find so engaging that it makes you lose all track of time. Why does it captivate you? To what or whom do you turn when you want to learn more?

Although these prompts might be similar to standard admissions essay questions, how an admissions committee reads a student's response is key. Instead of focusing on the student's writing, for example, the committee can choose to read, review, and make a decision based on the student's potential to persist or based on the need for specific interventions. If the institution expects students to stumble at some point during their college journeys, the committee could look for those students who can recognize challenges and determine what resources they need to overcome them. Additionally, if resilience, growth-mindset, and belonging interventions exist at the institution, the committee can look for students who might need these interventions to succeed in college.

Admissions interviews. Although essays can be good indicators of some aspects of students' abilities, an essay does not allow for the conversation the committee needs to get to know a student and to understand their specific challenges and needs. Asking questions about a student's experience can help them feel valued. It is possible to change some of the admissions criteria we use to evaluate applicants so that admissions decisions are made more equitably. With the admissions interview, students may have an opportunity to share their stories and experiences. An institution can expand the admissions criteria beyond test scores and grades by focusing on applicants' stories of resilience in the face of hardship.

Admissions committees can include an interview that focuses on questions to gauge the student's current sense of belonging, growth mindset, and resilience. The interview could include questions such as:

- What are your academic goals? What do you see as some of the biggest challenges in meeting those goals? What support would you need from an institution to help overcome those challenges?

- What do you need from an institution to feel like you belong?

Students' answers can help the institution connect the students with campus resources they might need before they even matriculate. When they do arrive, students can be reintroduced to these resources in meetings with advisors or during welcome week activities.

Keeping in mind that some students lack experience or expertise with interviewing and that some are not well equipped socially, the institution can forgo formal interviews in favor of informal admissions conversations. The idea is that the students share their experiences while giving the admissions committee an opportunity for follow-up questions.

Supplementing the application process with these approaches shifts the focus of admissions. Rather than acknowledging only artifacts that support the products of students' achievements (e.g., awards, high grades, test scores, letters of recommendation), admissions committees have an opportunity to acknowledge the processes by which students demonstrate a desire to learn and willingness to persist in the face of challenges.

Conditional admissions policies. Another opportunity to develop an institutional culture defined by and supportive of learning mindsets involves considering or reconsidering conditional admissions policies. Students may be admitted conditionally, for example, if their standardized test scores are below the cutoff but they are otherwise qualified—in which case, they may be required to take placement tests prior to registering for classes, participate in specialized academic support programs, or achieve a certain GPA in the first semester to maintain enrollment. As a result, conditional admissions may send the message that a student is not prepared or ready for college. Such messages affirm a fixed mindset and the "college is not for me" belief that many students have.

To remedy this, institutions should consider placing students in programs that address mindset and their sense of belonging in higher education. Such a program could be an extension of an FYE course that covers study skills, note-taking, or other tasks, or it could involve peer mentors. In the GRIT Coaching Program at the University of California, Los Angeles (UCLA, n.d.), students have the opportunity to work with a peer coach who has received more than 40 hours of training. Using the guiding principles of GRIT—guidance, resilience, integrity, and transformation—peer mentors work with students on stress/time management, study skills, communication skills, and more. Similar programs that pair an incoming student with someone close in age who has also experienced hardship can be created on any campus. For example, instead of students applying to work with peer coaches, as at UCLA, admissions committees could use answers from applicants' essays, interviews, or conversations to place at-risk students in this program after they gain admission.

David Laude is a chemistry professor at the University of Texas (UT) at Austin. When he was a student, Laude was much like Daniel, the focus of the mindset story earlier in this chapter. As a first-year student, Laude considered dropping out of school. Later, as a professor, he noticed some students were not doing well in his class and began to ask why. His question and his early experiences with college eventually led him to create the Texas Interdisciplinary Plan (TIP).

After reviewing the records of his former students, Laude noticed that those who failed his class either came from low-income families or had low SAT scores. In the fall of 1999, Laude reviewed the records of all his incoming students and identified those who were at risk of failing. He invited these 50 students to be a part of the new program. They would take Laude's chemistry class, but instead of being in a lecture hall of 500 students, they would be placed in classes of 30 students each. The smaller classes, coupled with a few hours of extra instruction and attention from advisors and peer mentors, produced tremendous results. Students in this program earned similar grades to those in the larger class sections, but they also persisted and graduated at a higher rate than the average UT student. These students got the extra help they needed, but more important, they became part of a community that helped them feel more connected to the school and more in tune with their academic potential (Tough, 2014).

The programs at UCLA and UT Austin were designed for at-risk students, and similar programs may benefit conditionally admitted students who are more likely to be at risk for academic problems. Another alternative to conditional admissions could be a program that encourages students to see potential in themselves they might not have recognized otherwise. Rather than being directly connected to a student's academic success, such a program might focus on addressing the whole student, so that they are better prepared for life after earning their degree. For example, Laude did not stop at TIP; he also developed the University Leadership Network (ULN), a scholarship program focused on leadership skills for selected students from low-income households and at risk of failing or not graduating from college. Students in ULN participate in community service and leadership workshops and are expected to dress in professional attire (Tough, 2014). The beauty of such programs is that students like Daniel have the opportunity to see themselves as something beyond their circumstances.

Messaging

How does an institution recruit those who want to study there and could benefit most from their educational experiences? The easiest way is to design messaging that supports learning mindsets—through the institution's mission statement; stories by students, faculty, and staff; and programs—in as many places as possible (e.g., social media, websites, billboards, commercials).

Recruiting material. When touting the entering class, institutions frequently emphasize student accomplishments, especially those related to academic performance (see Figure 5.1). These messages may become part of the recruiting materials used by the admissions staff. Creating a culture that moves beyond the standard messages about student achievement can start with rethinking the materials an institution uses to recruit and to reflect their students' success. The focus on academic achievement does not reflect learning mindsets and may send a message that undermines a sense of belonging for students who do not rise to the accomplishments of the average incoming first-year student. Emphasizing a 15% acceptance rate and the accomplishments of a select few (e.g., 32 valedictorians) sends a message of exclusion rather than inclusion. Moreover, the setbacks, challenges, and support experienced by successful students remains hidden because they are difficult to quantify.

Figure 5.2 offers an alternate way of describing an incoming class, one that reflects a culture committed to the importance of learning mindsets. The emphasis is on attitudes and behaviors that support academic success, such as challenging oneself, being resilient, or asking for help. It also normalizes setbacks (e.g., getting turned down for a team or having to rewrite a paper). Another feature of this revised incoming class data sheet is that it signals to students that the institution does not see them as "finished products" but as individuals who will experience challenge in the learning process.

Emails and letters to students. These can be formal ways to send students messages, and as such, they can seem more significant, especially if they come from a leader at the college. These messages can reinforce growth mindset by congratulating students for the effort they

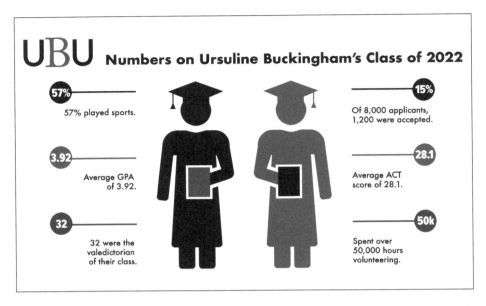

Figure 5.1. Sample recruitment message: Characteristics of Ursuline Buckingham's Class of 2022.

Figure 5.2. Reconfigured recruitment message for Ursuline Buckingham's Class of 2022.

are putting into their classes, for their academic performance, or for having reached certain milestones (e.g., credit hours, completion of core programs). Faculty can also email students if they see evidence of a shift in growth mindset or a demonstration of resilience in a class.

The Web and social media. Many students will encounter the institutional website before they ever step foot on the campus. Institution- and department-level pages should offer examples of growth or learning-focused mission statements in action by showcasing images of diverse learning, sharing student stories, and highlighting resources on resilience and learning mindsets.

Websites and social media channels can also offer messages about why students belong on campus, why they should persist, and how they can shift their mindsets. High Point University's Quality Enhancement Plan emphasized learning mindsets: "The university will employ best practices and encourage innovation across campus to help our students transition from a fixed to a growth mindset" (High Point University, n.d.). As part of the plan, which is also discussed in Chapter 7, High Point created a video called "What's the Point of College?" to communicate higher education's purpose. All incoming first-year students watch it. The university also combined quotes from the video with visuals to make the messages of growth mindset, resilience, and belonging more visible to students. Some of the quotes were, "Exams are supposed to make you struggle. So, if you are struggling, you are doing college right," "An easy class won't grow your intelligence," and "You are not your grades." In addition to such messages, colleges could use quotes from alumni or well-known individuals discussing their own resilience or growth mindsets:

- "Take chances, make mistakes. That's how you grow. Pain nourishes courage. You have to fail in order to practice being brave." (Mary Tyler Moore)

- "If you hear a voice within you say, 'You cannot paint,' then by all means paint, and that voice will be silenced." (Vincent Van Gogh)

- "You have to be able to accept failure to get better." (LeBron James)

Institutions can make such quotes visible to students in a variety of ways. Displaying them on posters around campus, as well as on social media, are subtle ways to promote the culture of the institution.

Course titles and offerings. Students will spend a majority of their time in class, and courses themselves send a message. Course titles at institutions reflect attitudes about belonging. What message is sent if, for example, no courses exploring works by non-White European authors (e.g., African American Literature, Mexican American Literature) are found on a schedule? Course titles that suggest current academic standing or ability (e.g., Developmental Math) may send the message to enrolled students they are not college material. Such messages could confirm beliefs a student already has about not belonging in college or might even contribute to a fixed mindset they have regarding their ability.

Course syllabi. Within the course itself, the messages students receive are also meaningful. In beginning to think about their ideal classroom environment, aspiring faculty attempt to answer questions such as:

- What are the roles and responsibilities of everyone in the classroom? What responsibility does the instructor have when a student is struggling with the content or fails an assignment? What responsibility does the student have?

- What classroom rules or policies will encourage and support a learning environment? How will the instructor ensure that all students feel their voices will be heard and respected?

- What types of regular activities or routines will be part of the learning experience? Will students be able to apply what they learn to their own lives? Will they have the opportunity to reflect on their growth and their efforts to learn in the course?

- How will assessment be used in the course? Is it designed to help students improve, or is its primary purpose to demonstrate what they can do?

Faculty can help establish a classroom culture geared toward growth mindset by answering these questions in their syllabi. Yet, sometimes the syllabus language may be so firm that it does not allow students opportunities to be resilient or develop a growth mindset. Statements such as "makeup exams will not be given," "late assignments will not be accepted," or "final course grade will be lowered for students who miss X number of classes" do not allow for the challenges that students face during a semester. Rather, they send the message that if "life happens" on exam day or the day an assignment is due, there is no opportunity to overcome the challenge or demonstrate resilience.

By contrast, the instructor can include statements that reinforce a commitment to academic resilience and a growth mindset such as the following:

- **Student responsibilities statement:** Participants enrolled in this course should continually monitor their learning, evaluate their own efforts, and actively seek help in a timely manner when needed. To successfully complete the course, students will need to assume an active role in the learning process by asking questions, completing assignments, and participating in discussions. In the event the student misses an assignment or due date, they should contact the instructor immediately to discuss opportunities to complete the task.

- **Instructor responsibilities statement:** It is my responsibility to help students grow and learn. This means I will provide clear instructions for all assignments, answer questions about the assignments, identify additional resources as necessary, provide review questions and study guides/activities for assessments (if appropriate), and provide rubrics and other criteria for evaluation of projects.

- **Growth mindset statement:** The goal of this class, and any college class you take, should not be to earn a particular grade. Instead, the goal is to learn something (or many things). If you have not learned anything and you earn an A, you have not really achieved academic success. Conversely, if you earn a C but have learned a wealth of knowledge, you have achieved something very, very valuable!

The grading policy listed in the syllabus can also encourage academic resilience. An instructor can provide opportunities for extra credit or for students to redo assignments or retake exams on which they performed poorly. Alternatively, they can provide resources to assist with certain assignments (e.g., library, tutoring center) or tools for students to access if they are having difficulty in the class (e.g., instructional videos, websites that provide further practice or additional instruction).

Merchandise and promotional items. Whether for sale or through giveaways, merchandise (e.g., T-shirts, pens, stress balls, water bottles) is a great avenue to encourage students to adopt learning mindsets. Students, faculty, and staff can submit slogans, artwork, or quotes for use on various items.

No matter the medium, institutions can send messages about the culture they promote. Those messages should primarily be positive and promote belonging. Institutions achieve this by making sure their message fits the audience.

Celebrating the Culture

Finally, in building a culture as educators, it is important to celebrate those walking in it already. What we support and who we recognize speaks to what we value as a culture. If we only celebrate winning athletic teams, those who make the dean's list, or those about to graduate, we might fail to recognize or validate the culture we are trying to create.

There is power in stories, which can transform how we perceive and interact with the world. Stories can inspire, motivate, educate, and move us. They can validate us and remind us that we are not alone. Allowing students to tell their stories of resilience, growth mindset, and belonging and sharing those stories with the larger community can encourage others. Sharing these stories on websites and on social media are also ways to reward students.

As another way to reinforce the culture, institutions can offer scholarships to students who demonstrate the school's mission. Colleges that hold awards ceremonies can consider awards for students who exemplify any one of these learning mindsets.

Conclusion

Educators should set the culture, then expect the culture. At some point, institutions do not have to announce who they are. Rather, they should demonstrate the culture through what they do and how they treat their students. If educators are not intentional and transparent about supporting belonging, growth mindset, and resilience, students like Daniel might not make it to higher education because it is not set up for them. On the other hand, if students get to college but do not receive the support promised by institutions, then higher education loses them. Institutional culture is rooted in beliefs—about ourselves as institutions, about our students' abilities, and about our responsibility to students. Changing that culture for the better does not stop with beliefs, however. We should be intentional about sharing those beliefs and using them to guide our actions, big and small.

Campus Conversations

The following questions are provided to begin conversations with key players on campus and as starting points for implementing change:

- What is our current mission statement, and how does it support belonging, growth mindset, and resilience? If it does not support these concepts, how can it be revised?

- What messages are we sending students? Are we exposing our students to messaging about belonging, growth mindset, and resilience? If so, how often? If not, how can we create supportive messages, and how often should we send messaging that addresses those things?

- What is the evidence that our institution supports belonging, growth mindset, and resilience beyond messaging?

Next Steps

The following steps are suggestions for moving from exploration to action:

1. Create or revise the institutional- or unit-level mission statement(s) to include language about belonging, growth mindset, and resilience.

2. Create a strategic plan that identifies and addresses the changes needed in the application processes for both employment and admissions.

3.   Create a strategic plan for how to approach sending messages to students and how and when to celebrate students who exhibit learning mindsets and resilience.

4.   Identify new and existing initiatives or programs that will promote this new culture and ramp them up, if needed.

References

Goldstein, D. (2017, September 17). When affirmative action isn't enough. *The New York Times*. Retrieved from https://www.nytimes.com/2017/09/17/us/affirmative-action-college.html

High Point University. (n.d). *Quality Enhancement Plan.* Retrieved April 22, 2019, from Quality Enhancement Plan homepage, http://www.highpoint.edu/qep/

Jaschik, S. (2018a, April 16). Where colleges recruit … and where they don't. *Inside Higher Ed.* Retrieved from https://www.insidehighered.com/admissions/article/2018/04/16/study-analyzes-where-colleges-recruit-and-where-they-dont

Jaschik, S. (2018b, December 3). The impact of holistic admissions. *Inside Higher Ed.* Retrieved from https://www.insidehighered.com/admissions/article/2018/12/03/lsu-has-moved-holistic-admissions-finding-increased-diversity-and

Tough, P. (2014, May 15). Who gets to graduate? *The New York Times*. Retrieved from www.nytimes.com/2014/05/18/magazine/who-gets-to-graduate.html

The University of California, Los Angeles. (n.d.). *Welcome to the GRIT coaching program!* Retrieved April 22, 2019, from UCLA GRIT Coaching Program homepage, www.grit.ucla.edu/

Yeager, D. S., & Walton, G. M. (2011). Social-psychological interventions in education: They're not magic. *Review of Educational Research, 81* (2), 267-301.

Chapter 6

Professional Development to Foster Belonging, Growth Mindset, and Resilience

Latoya Lewis

Lisette's Learning Mindset Story: Growth Through Opportunity

"Miss, you should run for president. If you can handle us, you can definitely run the country." This is what Tiana, one of her very first students, told Lisette in 2004, the year Lisette began teaching. As a New York City teaching fellow, she was placed in one of Harlem's highest-need high schools to teach a high-needs subject. The training she received as a fellow prepared her to engage struggling students.

Throughout her years as a teacher in Harlem, Lisette experienced many moments when she did not feel like she was making a difference, and trying to fix all of the problems her students faced was challenging. Despite these moments, however, Lisette always felt like a teacher, and she could see herself teaching until it was time to retire. So Tiana's comment caught her off guard. Tiana saw something other than a teacher in Lisette, and although the remark was flattering, Lisette did not entertain the idea. She simply did not believe that she wanted to be, or even that she could be, anything else.

But Tiana saw Lisette as a leader, and Lisette's future colleagues and supervisors echoed the sentiment. Although no one else thought Lisette could be president, many asked, "When are you going to be a principal?" or said she would make a good administrator. When she took a job in higher education, it did not take long for people to ask Lisette to serve in leadership roles where she could help evaluate adjunct instructors, build and schedule courses, and lead training sessions for faculty.

Still, she rejected the idea of being anything other than a teacher. One reason she eschewed a leadership role was that she had accepted many negative beliefs about administrators: They were on education's dark side. Out of touch, they did not really understand the plight of teachers or students. To the extent that they focused on student success, it was for the sake of performance indicators—not the students themselves. In addition, Lisette did not feel that she had leadership ability. "I can't lead people," she thought. "I can't supervise; I can't manage anything." Her beliefs about administrators and her lack of belief in herself kept Lisette from actively pursuing a leadership position—for a while.

When it came to teaching, Lisette had a growth mindset, believing that her students' learning could grow with effort, time, and resources. She truly wanted them to have access to education, so she invested many hours outside the classroom creating lessons, assignments, and activities that would reach each student. But when she thought about being a leader, she had a fixed mindset. Her expectations for how far she could go as an educator, and how she thought about leaders, were very limited.

When a colleague went on sick leave, Lisette had a chance to serve as interim department chair for one academic year. After having served as lead faculty for several years, Lisette accepted the position because she had prior experience performing certain chair duties and because it would not be permanent. However, once taking over in the role, Lisette began to realize she could perform the duties. She brought her own style to the position, something that made the transition enjoyable. She began to see how she could use her new role to reach students beyond the ones she was teaching.

Though she was happy when her colleague was well enough to return, Lisette desired more responsibilities as a leader. She read books on education and leadership, met weekly with other leaders who were reading the same books, participated in leadership development, and worked with mentors who coached her. With every book, meeting, program, and coaching session, Lisette began to see her definition of leader expand. She started to understand that there were ineffective and effective leaders. In pursuing opportunities to develop her understanding, Lisette not only saw herself as a leader but also learned skills and strategies to be a more effective one. The chance to do the work and the professional development opportunities she received had shifted her mindset about her leadership abilities.

Defining Professional Development

Professional development can help employees advance in their careers, but ultimately it helps them understand how to do their jobs better. Whether it involves reading books, attending conferences or workshops, or working one-on-one with a mentor, anything we do in an effort to be more effective in our roles is professional development. In higher education, where the ultimate goal is helping students succeed, it is important that institutions provide professional development opportunities that teach faculty and staff how to develop, work toward, and engage in an environment focused on creating and then supporting learning mindsets.

As humans, we naturally learn about our culture by watching others who have been in the culture the longest. Our family environments provide an example. As children, we learn what to eat, how to speak, and how to behave from the examples of our parents, grandparents, and other adults in the family. In cultures where an older generation is harder to define, individuals learn the preferred norms and values by watching those who have engaged in the culture the longest.

When students enter college, they learn what is acceptable and expected in that culture by watching the experts—those who have already learned the culture and can serve as role models. Although lectures and presentations might be ways to learn about culture, students learn more through their interactions with people at the institution. For this reason, it is important and necessary to train those who work directly with students so that faculty, staff, and administrators promote a culture that supports belonging, growth mindset, and resilience.

To help create models and train faculty and staff to work with students, two types of professional development are needed. The first focuses on helping faculty and staff develop their own sense of belonging, growth mindset, and resilience. By experiencing what they will later ask their students to commit to, faculty and staff can become experts in the culture. Those who have developed these traits are in a better position to facilitate the same process in students. The second type of professional development focuses on teaching faculty and staff how to help students develop belonging, growth mindset, and resilience. This training is specific to the different departments that serve students in a variety of ways.

Before rolling out any learning opportunities, those responsible for professional development at an institution have to devise a strategic plan. It should include what the development will cover and how it will be designed, as well as how training will be made available to faculty and staff. When crafting a professional development plan, the institution should examine current beliefs and begin to look at those who will bring the vision to life. During the plan's first year, it is important to establish a framework before the work involving many employees begins. Getting the institution's leaders on board early is also vital.

The initial professional development plan could address such topics as:

- data that support and/or promote a learning mindset,
- common language that will be used by all employees and students at the institution, and
- role-specific development.

For each topic, the institution should design training and development that will answer questions related to both what (the content or rationale for programs) and how (method of delivery). Table 6.1. offers a template for creating a professional development plan. The specifics of professional development design for each of these topics will be discussed in greater detail in the sections that follow.

With respect to organizing professional development, large meetings, where all employees are present, are key. Such meetings are opportunities to inform about the culture that the institution is promoting and are good settings to provide an overview of where the institution is and where it intends to go. It is important that everyone knows this vision so that when professional development opportunities arise, employees will know why they participate. During these sessions, the data and the common language the institution is using can be introduced.

Table 6.1
Sample Professional Development Plan for Institutions

Session	Description of sessions	Goals of the sessions	Stakeholders	Timeline for delivering to faculty and staff
Data	Content			
	Delivery			
Common language	Content			
	Delivery			
Role-specific development	Content			
	Delivery			

Regular professional development can also be offered through short videos and lunch-and-learns, for example, to remind people of the language and its context. Faculty and staff can share their own understanding of the direction the institution is going; in doing so, people can see their role in helping make the vision a reality.

Using Data to Support Learning Mindsets

Content

Frequently, the first step in professional development efforts is to establish the value proposition. Questions that might drive this type of content include, Why is this work important or necessary? What concepts will help create a culture of belonging, growth mindset, and resilience? What should we focus on to achieve our desired results? What work needs to be done to move toward this culture?

To get employees, especially faculty, on board with any initiative, it is important to provide data and research that explain why a focus on growth mindset and belonging is meaningful. A useful starting point is the institution's goals or key priorities. How close is the institution to meeting those priorities? Whether the answer is near to or far from such targets, learning mindsets can be a factor. Sessions on institutional priorities might present research on learning mindsets and highlight how such approaches can help the institution meet its targets. For example, if persistence is a priority, how can fostering learning mindsets facilitate higher persistence rates among students? These sessions might also feature case studies from peer institutions that have faced similar challenges and have succeeded with programs and interventions to address these challenges. Examples include programs such as the University of Texas at Austin's Texas Interdisciplinary Plan and the University Leadership Network, both described in Chapter 5.

Another way to get employees invested is to help them understand how they can contribute to the larger picture. How do their own mindsets contribute to or hinder students' success? Institutions can also collect data on employees' mindsets and discuss how they affect the performance of the institution and the students.

Delivery

When data are presented about the institution and its students, institutional goals are set, and because all faculty and staff are asked to take part in an initiative concerned with building a new culture, it is important that all employees receive this information. Convocations, state-of-the-college presentations, and president's forums are all appropriate examples of settings for this type of messaging. Such sessions are good opportunities to analyze how the professional development offerings will help the institution meet its goals, to preview the professional development plan, describe how it will help the institution meet its goals, highlight who will be involved, and let staff know how they can participate.

Finding a Common Language

Content

What do we mean by belonging, growth mindset, and resilience? Each of these terms has varying definitions, and people might think of them in very different, even contradictory, ways because their understanding might be limited or flawed. Students cannot demonstrate these qualities without a clear understanding of them or models to emulate. Unless everyone at an institution understands these concepts, a culture for nurturing and developing them will not thrive. Therefore, how an institution interprets and approaches learning mindsets is important.

If faculty and staff are to model learning mindsets, an institution needs consistent messaging about them. When choosing the language to describe such mindsets, institutions should consider possible nuances for some of the terms as well as specific differences to be addressed across the institution. For example, whereas resilience might refer to bouncing back from any challenge, Stoltz (2015) extended the definition to include leveraging adversity to achieve one's most worthy goals. Similarly, Duckworth (2016) defined grit as the passion and perseverance it takes to achieve long-term goals, whereas Stoltz suggested it is the ability to do whatever it takes, even make sacrifices, to achieve our most desired goals. Once the parties involved understand the terminology, the institution can provide a framework for its mission, vision, and values as they relate to belonging, growth mindset, and resilience.

Delivery

The institution should provide several opportunities for combined sessions so faculty and staff can learn the common language pertaining to qualities such as growth mindset. This way, all parties can collectively receive the same message and terminology and begin to adopt them. Short (30-minute) lunch-and-learns allow faculty and staff to discuss the terminology and how to apply it to their daily roles. Lecture series, with sessions generally an hour in length, provide opportunities for faculty, staff, and administrators to define and discuss messaging. To help new faculty and staff, who might begin work after the institution has already developed a foundation for such language, learning mindsets should be introduced during the onboarding process. Employee orientation is an ideal time to share the data, assessments, and language.

Although it is important that all faculty and staff participate in professional development, subtle approaches, rather than mandates, might be most effective. Such development need not be limited to classrooms and lecture halls. The institution could post short, informative videos to its website or share them on social media. One- to two-minute videos, filmed like mini commercials, can remind employees of the common language or of examples that highlight belonging, growth mindset, and resilience.

Another idea is to celebrate (e.g., in newsletters, meetings, social media) the behaviors faculty and staff already exhibit that exemplify learning mindsets. Each time an institution does this, it has an opportunity to use the common language around growth mindset and remind people of those definitions and the culture. Each celebration can emphasize examples of the behaviors we hope to instill and encourage. Along with being reminders of the common language, celebrations also serve as real examples of growth mindset, resilience, and belonging.

The more an institution's employees experience the common language around these qualities, the more opportunities they have to become familiar with them. Using the language consistently helps it to become a part of an institution's identity.

Role-Specific Development

Content

Earlier, we mentioned that people really learn how to fit into a culture by watching those who are already experts in that culture. For that to happen in higher education, institutions must help faculty and staff develop the behaviors they want to encourage in students—including a sense of belonging, growth mindset, and resilience. Either before beginning professional development or in conjunction with it, faculty and staff should examine their current beliefs and how these can contribute to students' successes or failures. Taking these steps is important because institutions cannot expect students to become what they do not see. Once faculty and staff understand who they are, they can begin to explore their perceptions of their students. Some questions for faculty and staff to keep in mind include:

- Do students feel as if they belong at the institution? If so, what evidence points to their sense of belonging? If not, what programs and resources can be put into place to help encourage this?

- How do we see our students—as victims who need to be hand-held or as individuals who are capable but might need a bit more motivation? In other words, do we see our students as resilient?

Academic departments and student services units can come together to explore their own understanding of belonging, growth mindset, and resilience while also assessing those qualities in themselves. This work can lay the groundwork for more specialized training on promoting belonging and resilience and encouraging a growth mindset in specific roles on campus. For faculty, such training should involve creating a classroom environment that promotes each of these traits. Students' physical environment is a factor, but so are assignments and activities that keep these traits in mind. Employees who work in student services can also be strong supporters and encouragers of learning mindsets. For example, an academic advisor or counselor might be tasked with talking to a student who is ready to drop a class because they have a fixed mindset or lack resilience. Those who work in student life can focus their training on the types of clubs and organizations their institution could create to ensure all students are represented and have a voice.

Delivery

Team meetings do not usually focus on professional development, but they can help further an institutional staff's understanding of belonging, growth mindset, and resilience. For example, teams could integrate a "mindset moment" at the beginning or end of meetings, where a designated team member knows in advance that they will be responsible for sharing how they have shown belonging, growth mindset, or resilience. Such moments can also be ways to celebrate employees who are guided by learning mindsets. Faculty and staff can share about the challenges they face in their roles and what it means to have a growth mindset or be resilient in light of these challenges.

To start a meeting, groups at an institution could use icebreakers that focus on belonging, growth mindset, and resilience. In Human Bingo, a common example, everyone in the meeting gets a bingo card showing questions or statements related to things people have done or experienced. Participants must then interview people in the room, with the aim of finding those who have done or experienced the items on their card. When they do, they write the person's name in the square, continuing until they get four or five in a row (and hence, bingo).

Because a number of people likely will have some of the same experiences, this icebreaker promotes belonging. Some examples of these statements include *is an only child*, *played sports in high school*, and *listens to country music* among others. Faculty and staff may be able to identify with several of these statements, and as they play the game, they can find others who have similar experiences. The statements could also relate to growth mindset or resilience, such as *was a first-generation college student*, *took the SAT or ACT more than once*, and *recently overcame a hardship*. Statements such as these may be shared experiences, and they can also be evidence that a person has demonstrated a growth mindset or resilience.

Brain teasers can be used to engage staff members and can also lead to conversations about mindset and resilience. For example, a rebus puzzle, which uses letters and symbols to illustrate a common phrase or saying, can be challenging, but it also allows people to discuss how they had to persist or change their way of thinking to solve the puzzle. Getting people to share stories or work together as a team to solve a problem can encourage belonging.

Idea shares, usually run by a professional development team, can also be created and run by faculty and staff. During these sessions, spanning 30 to 90 minutes, faculty and staff share strategies, best practices, stories, and lessons about embedding belonging, growth mindset, and resilience into their learning environments. Unlike a workshop, in which one or two people are responsible for sharing ideas for the session, these discussions can be BYOI (bring your own idea) style, in which every participant has the chance to share a strategy or story.

During workshops, faculty and staff not only can hear about how to incorporate growth mindset, resilience, and belonging into their areas, but they can also create something for immediate use in promoting that culture. If faculty and staff are learning about what makes a good mindset story, for example, they can begin working on their own stories during the workshop. If advisors are learning about best practices for talking to students in danger of withdrawing, sessions could allow time for advisors to respond to scenarios or to write their own scripts or conversation starters.

A More Intensive Approach

These methods are subtle, and institutions can facilitate them in various ways, but an institution might also seek more intensive programs. Unlike a one-shot workshop, an intensive program spans a significant amount of time (e.g., semester, academic year), during which participants are working to become experts on a subject. A certification program, for example, allows participants to apply what they are learning in the course to their classroom teaching or other work with students. At the program's end, participants should produce some sort of artifact demonstrating their work. If the institution develops a certification program for growth mindset, for example, what options will be available for ongoing training or recertification beyond the initial professional development program?

The Instructional Technology Certification Program (Lewis, 2017) is one example. This program, designed by a faculty member, teaches other faculty how to introduce instructional technologies in the classroom. Over the course of an academic year, a cohort of faculty meet nine times for three-hour sessions. Each session focuses on one topic, and participants engage with multiple technology tools. The participants then choose a tool that best fits their teaching style to integrate into their classes. In each session, participants discuss challenges they are facing, thereby supporting one another in their goals for instructional technology. At the end of the year, participants create a portfolio of the tools they have incorporated into their classes. As part of a presentation, they share final reflections about their growth in the program as well as their greatest takeaways.

Although this program does not address learning mindsets explicitly, it does help to develop participants' learning mindsets. First, because the program introduces a variety of technology tools, instructors begin to see their definitions of teaching and of technology grow. By using technology, they build confidence and expand their ability in the classroom, and students get to see their instructors trying something new. Participants also become more resilient, as learning new technology is challenging, and many make mistakes in the process.

Through facing and overcoming the challenge of learning something new, participants take lessons they can pass on to their students. Such programs have the added benefit of helping build community in the classroom, as the instructor learns something new and can then better relate to students in the class.

Key Principles for Professional Development Plans

- Connect all professional development offerings to the mission, vision, and values of the institution. Each of these aspects provides a framework for the campus culture. Aligning offerings to the institution's beliefs helps ensure the training is effective.

- When designing professional development workshops, application has to be a key consideration. Participants need to be able to connect what they are learning to the institution or to the culture. The end goal is not simply to know about culture but to be able to shape culture. How can participants take what they have learned and apply it immediately to their work, or how can the training itself be an application exercise? For example, is a video that teaches the common language for promoting growth mindset applicable to anything that currently exists at the institution?

- Before designing sessions for professional development, determine how faculty and staff understand their roles, and create opportunities for them to see the possibilities of those roles. Professional development cannot be productive if participants have a fixed mindset about what they do. If a faculty member believes teaching means lecturing only, for example, or if an advisor believes advising involves only registering students for classes, professional development that goes against these views could create resistance. What faculty and staff get from professional development is connected to the beliefs and experiences they bring with them. Therefore, professional development that works with a growth mindset is key. If a session focuses on a specific topic, include multiple options for approaching the topic. For example, a session on encouraging a growth mindset through conversations should not cover just one strategy; given a variety of approaches, participants can choose the best fit for how they interact with students. If only one strategy is given, participants should have the chance to practice adapting the strategy to fit their own styles. Then, it becomes more authentic when used with students. Providing options during professional development also makes it harder for naysayers, who might feel the strategies will not work in their areas, to dismiss them.

- Provide opportunities for employees to reflect on their learning. Content from professional development could be new and challenging for employees, so they will need space to discuss what they take from it. Through reflection activities, employees can demonstrate resilience by talking about the challenges they face (Lischka, Barlow, Willingham, Hartland, & Stephens, 2015).

- Not all professional development needs to be about learning mindsets. Because there is no one way to help develop learning mindsets, professional development that offers a one-size-fits-all approach removes the opportunity for employees to learn. Instead, allow faculty to try new things. According to Dress (2016, Create a culture, para. 2),

> If we want to grow as teachers, we have to be willing to make mistakes on a regular basis. When mistakes are accepted as something that even skilled teachers do, they are more likely to be embraced as learning opportunities.

Professional development should embrace experimentation, as this type of training also helps promotes growth. Table 6.2 offers a template for an individual professional development plan that allows individuals to customize their own learning and development needs.

Table 6.2
Individual Development Plan

Specific goal	Specific actions or professional development offerings to achieve the goal	How does this goal align with the culture of the institution?	Anticipated date of completion	Status (initiated, in-progress, completed)	Comments
Learn how to infuse concepts of grit into my courses.	*Attend Grit Summit at Lone Star College-Tomball.*	*The institution is committed to helping students graduate on time. Resilience in the classroom can be an intervention to assist students.*	*November 2020*	*Initiated*	

Conclusion

Chapter 5 focuses on creating a campus culture that supports belonging, growth mindset, and resilience. Is the institution trying to create a culture that supports belonging, growth mindset, and resilience, or is the institution training its people to support these concepts? An institution cannot simply become the culture by trying; it has to train people by offering professional development that helps everyone understand the culture, creates a shared purpose, gets buy-in, connects people to the institution, and prepares and equips faculty and staff for the work they will actually do. Professional development should do all of these things, and if planned well and implemented effectively, it can cultivate excitement around what it will take to change the culture.

Campus Conversations

The following questions are provided to begin conversations with key players on campus and as starting points for implementing change:

- Who or what program, office, or department is responsible for professional development at our institution?

- What types of professional development are offered, and how do those offerings reinforce or undermine the research on learning mindsets and belonging?

- What types of professional development offerings might be well received at our institution? What types of sessions will work well, and which will not work?

Next Steps

The following steps are suggestions for moving from exploration to action:

1. Determine the language or messaging the institution will use in terms of learning mindsets and belonging.

2. Encourage professional development team members to meet with other departments to begin building specialized training sessions.

3. Develop a strategic plan that addresses the what, the how, and the types of professional development the institution will offer. See Tables 6.1 and 6.2 for examples.

References

Dress, A. (2016, March/April). Adopting a growth mindset. *Exchange.* Retrieved from https://www.childcareexchange.com/article/adopting-a-growth-mindset/5022812/

Duckworth, A. (2016). *Grit: The power of passion and perseverance.* New York, NY: Scribner.

Lewis, L. (2017). Technology in the classroom: Instructional technology certification program increases engagement. *NISOD Innovation Abstracts, 39*(13).

Lischka, A. E., Barlow, A. T., Willingham, J. C., Hartland, K., & Stephens, D. C. (2015). Mindset in professional development: Exploring evidence of different mindsets. *Proceedings of the 37th annual meeting of the North American chapter of the International Group for the Psychology of Mathematics in Education.* East Lansing, MI: Michigan State University.

Stoltz, P. G. (2015). *GRIT: The new science of what it takes to persevere, flourish, succeed.* San Luis Obispo, CA: ClimbStrong Press.

Chapter 7

Creating an Assessment Plan for Learning-Mindset Interventions

Amy Baldwin

Richard's Mindset Story: Using Assessment to Broaden Impact

As director of a federally funded program, Richard is charged with improving outcomes among a small population of students who come from disadvantaged backgrounds. Historically, the institution has served academically gifted students who went on to become CEOs for Fortune 500 companies, judges, and community philanthropists. In an effort to increase the diversity of the student body, the institution sought and won a grant for a program to support low-income first-generation students, yet according to institutional data, these students are the least likely to persist and graduate.

The program has had some success since its inception: Although the number of students served each year is small, they receive wrap-around support (e.g., intrusive advising and tutoring), they make positive academic progress, and they are retained each semester. The first few cohorts have met, but not quite exceeded, the graduation rate that is part of the grant's assessment plan.

Despite the program's past successes, Richard believes his student participants could achieve more than the modest improvements he is bound to meet through the grant. In fact, he thinks a growth-mindset and belonging intervention could help close the achievement gaps between his students and the rest of the campus population. What concerns him is uncertainty about whether the rest of the university will buy into his ideas for improving outcomes for all students. He feels his standalone program would be best served if the students and strategies were better integrated into the larger university's strategic plan. As he aims to improve outcomes for his students and assesses the effectiveness of potential interventions, Richard has some questions to explore:

- What new goals does he have?
- What can he do to revise how student outcomes are assessed?
- What data will he need to collect?
- If he can demonstrate significant improvements in his students' success, how can he share those results in a way that might convince the university to do more for all its students?

A Fixed Mindset About Assessment

For many in higher education, assessment is a dirty word. These educators might say, "If we could just do our jobs and not worry about assessment, all would be right with the world." Others may complain that they do not learn anything new from assessment, that they are unsure how to do it, or that no one pays attention to the results. About 20 years ago, a department chair told me that assessment was an "educational fad" and would be on its way out in no time, making way for yet another campus initiative. I knew even then that assessment was not a fad, but rather the underpinning of what we do as educators. We just had to get better at recognizing and refining the process we use to determine whether something works. We also needed to recognize that assessment and evaluation are two different practices in higher education that sometimes get lumped together. Because assessment is process-oriented and focused on learning, it differs from evaluation, which is product-oriented and focused on making a value judgment.

Assessment does not have to be feared. It might just require a different mindset to realize its value as an exercise. In fact, the process of assessment shares characteristics with growth mindset, belonging, and resilience: The challenges are opportunities to improve the questions asked, the data collected, the interpretation of the data, and the dissemination of results. Here are some other points to remember about the process:

- It is common to feel directionless at first, but it does get easier with practice.
- Many people who find assessment to be challenging seek help and find that the resources they access lead to improvement.
- When a program or intervention is not meeting its goals, it is important to examine the reasons why and make changes based on the data.

In short, the thoughts that many students have about college are similar to those we may have when confronting assessment. Nonetheless, assessment is essentially about improvement—making a plan to improve, deciding how much we want to improve, executing a plan, demonstrating the results of our improvement plan, and, finally, making changes to the plan to improve more.

Another way to consider assessment in light of the learning-mindset interventions discussed in previous chapters is to think about how it should be integral to an intervention. Indeed, it should guide the intervention in terms of where to focus the doses of growth mindset and belonging. Obviously, assessment should measure the progress of students and the effectiveness of intervention. Ultimately, good assessment is intervention.

Asking the Right Questions

After reading the preceding chapters, we hope readers are excited about the possibilities for effecting change on their campuses, yet we know that enthusiasm alone will not be enough to get an intervention or initiative off the ground, let alone build it into a sustainable model that can have an impact on generations of students. It is wise, then, to start any assessment plan by discussing a set of questions with key stakeholders in the project.

What goals are we trying to achieve? Goals should be tied to assessment data that point to opportunities to boost or eliminate gaps in student success. For example, the institution may seek to reduce the achievement gap between students of color and White students in first-year gateway courses. For some, the easiest path to ensuring higher student success outcomes might be to change the types of students who are admitted; however, this approach is not possible or desirable for most campuses. In that case, the institution may need to engage in a serious conversation about how to align institutional goals with what research tells us about supporting success for a wider range of students. Such a conversation might yield the following goal: Reduce by half or eliminate the 10% achievement gap for students of color in gateway courses by implementing belonging interventions.

What kind of intervention should we use? Answering this question entails a review of the research to see how other institutions have tried to achieve similar goals, some of which are explored in earlier chapters of this volume. It could also involve searching for potential models. For example, High Point University's Quality Enhancement Plan (QEP; High Point University, n.d.) infuses growth mindset into the culture and fabric of the institution. Along with changing the culture, the QEP covers training faculty and staff in the principles and practices of growth mindset, giving students information and opportunities to demonstrate growth mindset, and assessing levels of growth mindset and grit in employees and students. Although not every institution will choose such a comprehensive set of interventions for its first project, the strategies High Point employed for its QEP provide insight into how to adopt a comprehensive focus on learning mindsets.

After determining what kind of intervention to use, questions about the timing, the occasion for the intervention, and the duration should be the next steps of this discussion. Answering these questions thoroughly will take repeated meetings with constituents, solid leadership, and maybe even revisiting the initial question. Once an intervention is selected, part of the conversation should include the question, *Are we implementing the intervention correctly?* In other words, is the institution being faithful to recommendations from the research, or does the reality of implementation require some modifications? One way to ensure that the intervention is faithfully implemented is to review pilot phase results to see if they are in line with what is expected based on previous research studies. If results seem wildly different or move in the opposite direction, (e.g., making an achievement gap wider), then it is worth exploring the implementation processes for potential problems.

Finally, ***How will we know the intervention is successful?*** is a question that should lead institutions to discuss the measures they will use to identify changes in student achievement or behavior—if they have occurred. This question should be explicitly tied back to the first question regarding goals. If we look at the example goal of reducing the achievement gaps between students of color and White students in first-year courses, then a successful intervention would be one that reduced or eliminated the gap.

Going back to Richard, he has two goals in mind: (a) to improve the outcomes of his program's participants significantly by using a growth-mindset and belonging intervention, and (b) to scale the intervention to the entire student population. The goal that Richard has the most influence over at this point is the first one. He will be best served by using the questions in the following section to build his assessment plan.

Revisiting Astin's I-E-O Model for Assessing Learning Mindsets

As described in the introduction, Astin's (1991) I-E-O model is a good place to start when thinking about assessment, and it may provide an opportunity to rethink the key concepts. Inputs, such as students' demographic information and achievements prior to entering college, have been standard ways to measure or designate students' characteristics, and it is likely that institutions will continue to ask for students' race/ethnicity, gender, first-generation status, high school GPA, and other descriptive data. We hope, however, to call for a rethinking of the inclusion of some inputs (e.g., standardized test scores) and the exclusion of others (e.g., narrative about overcoming a challenge). Indeed, many institutions have gone "test optional," meaning they no longer require students to submit ACT or SAT scores as part of their admissions packet (Strauss, 2017). This change in admissions practices sets the stage for institutions to reconsider the kinds of data they collect about incoming first-year students. See Chapter 5, Figures 5.1 and 5.2, for examples of this kind of change in data collection and reporting.

Learning More About Inputs

One of the first places to gather data to inform discussions on learning mindsets is an institution's admissions office. Using admissions data can prompt questions that align with the principles of growth mindset, belonging, and resilience and can reflect a focus on inclusivity and support. Topics and questions that would help an institution create a richer picture of an incoming class include:

- **First-generation student status.** Are you the first in your immediate family to attend college? Will you be the first to graduate from college?

- **Setbacks that end in comebacks.** Describe a time when you experienced a challenge that you eventually overcame.

- **Support networks.** Who are the people in your life who have contributed to your success?

- **Challenges that increase learning.** Describe a time when you were challenged to learn something and improved through practice.

Although most of these questions ask for qualitative data, those who compile admissions information could convert the answers to quantitative data points by providing numbers or percentages of students who identify challenges, support, and improved learning in their pre-college experiences. See Chapter 5 for a more detailed discussion of how to create a more inclusive admissions process.

To capture data from the student narratives, the institution could implement some of the growth-mindset and belonging interventions discussed in previous chapters. For example, after students read or watch stories about previous students overcoming challenges, they could be invited to share their concerns about the college experience and discuss strategies to address them. Institutions can ask students' permission to share the data as part of the incoming class profile or to use selected stories in other publications. When based on data that signal resilience, the conversations about incoming classes that faculty, staff, and administrators have would shift dramatically away from those that weigh grades, test scores, and extracurricular involvement.

As for Richard's desire to rethink his assessment plan for his program participants, he will need to continue collecting the data that the federal government requires colleges to report, but he could also include questions such as those mentioned here to provide a more robust description of students admitted through his program. Moreover, he could use the information to develop some baseline data showing his students' resilience.

Understanding Educational Environments

The second part of Astin's I-E-O model is environment, which includes an institution's culture, programs, policies, and even expectations of its students. The college environment is where we often start thinking about how to influence learning mindsets; it also is where much of the research on learning-mindset interventions has occurred, even if those interventions occurred pre-matriculation. An institution's environment is often described in physical, tangible terms (e.g., a program of study, a physical location, an emphasis on liberal studies). However, we argue that an invisible environment—one that can be influenced by growth-mindset, belonging, and resilience interventions—has a greater influence on student success. This invisible environment refers to how students feel in spaces on campus as an effect of the physical environment or of the messages they receive about their belonging. Do they see others like themselves represented in media and communications from the institution, in the classroom, and in the social spaces on campus?

Expanding the Scope of College Outcomes

Typical outcomes such as persistence and graduation rates are important for all institutions, but often we focus on them with little consideration for how subtle changes in the environment, such as creating a culture that promotes growth mindset, can affect student outcomes significantly. What other kinds of outcomes could institutions consider in addition to retention, persistence, and graduation? Certainly, we can use other measures to determine the effectiveness of learning-mindset interventions. Following are some to consider for those beginning a conversation on effective interventions:

- **Satisfactory academic progress (e.g., earning 67% of attempted credits during a term).** How many students maintain satisfactory academic progress each semester? Are there any significant differences between groups who participate in an intervention and those who do not?

- **Time to degree.** How quickly are students completing their degrees? Are there improvements in four-year and six-year graduation rates for students who have completed an intervention?

- **Probationary/suspension status.** What percentage of students are on probation or have been recommended for suspension? Are there trends to note for students who have completed an intervention?

- **Campus connections.** How do students rate their sense of belonging and engagement with the campus? Do any groups seem less engaged or less satisfied with how they fit in?

- **Tutoring/supplemental instruction/peer coaching.** At what rates do students use academic and personal support services such as tutoring, supplemental instruction, and peer coaching? How has that usage trended?

- **GPA.** What are the GPAs of certain groups in the cohort of first-year students? Are there any significant differences among the groups?

- **Loneliness/homesickness.** What percentage of first-year students indicate feeling lonely or homesick in the first semester? Are there any differences in subgroups?

Of course, many more possibilities for outcomes may be of interest to the institution. A good strategy, at least initially, is to consider outcomes that can be assessed quickly and preferably within the first semester. In Richard's case, he already tracks satisfactory academic progress, fall-to-spring and fall-to-fall retention, and graduation rates. He could also choose to include GPA and campus connections to determine whether a growth-mindset and belonging intervention affects those outcomes.

Collecting and Interpreting the Data

When collecting and interpreting the data related to an intervention, it is important to remember that not all data are created equal, nor are they equally available. Assessment plans might need to address whether requests have to be vetted through institutional research processes and procedures. For example, Richard's plan to use GPA as an outcome for his growth-mindset and belonging intervention means he will need to work with his institutional research office to request the data. If he decides to collect data on campus connections by providing students with a survey of student engagement and relationships, he may be required to submit an application to the institutional review board (IRB) for approval. Whether he collects data on his own or goes through a research office, he will need to consider the security issues inherent in the process of requesting, accessing, and reviewing student academic records.

After collecting the data, the next steps are to review, analyze, discuss, question, and interpret the information available on student behaviors, habits, mindsets, and performance. Additional questions that can guide interpretation include:

- What conclusions can be drawn from the data? Are there any trends, and are those positive or negative?
- What additional questions do the data raise?
- What other information might be needed?
- What are the implications for practice, and what policy decisions can be made based on the data?
- How well did the intervention work? Are some students not being reached, or needs not being met?

A robust investigation of the data will inevitably yield additional ideas, questions, and concerns. Program managers should capture such questions, explore them with others who can provide insight to possible answers, and determine which ones to explore further. In this chapter's opening story, Richard could take his survey data—in which his program participants rated their engagement more highly than students who were not participating in the program—to various departments on campus to gain insights into why that occurred.

Good Assessment Informs Action

A good assessment plan can inform action and positive change, but we all know that too many assessment plans sit in three-ring binders in a filing cabinet, never to be seen again. In some cases, the plan was too unwieldy, involved too many steps and people, or did not align clearly with the institution's overall mission or strategic plan. Richard hopes a change within his program will influence the campus at large, even though he does not occupy a position at the institution that could make such a change for the entire campus. That said, some strategies Richard could employ to influence campus culture include:

- reporting the outcomes of the intervention, even if the results are modest;
- sharing methods and practices with various campus groups and building consensus around a common goal of student success;
- identifying key players and potential allies with similar goals for the students or their programs; and
- addressing pushback appropriately while conceding to the limitations of the interventions.

It is natural to get excited by significant results and to be frustrated by the slow pace of change in higher education. On the surface, an assessment plan can seem to be an exercise in making small changes slowly, but it can provide the stability and forward movement needed to make positive change, even if incremental.

Conclusion

Because of their simple design, the research on and recommendations for creating a culture that embraces growth mindset, belonging, and resilience shared in previous chapters have rightfully garnered interest and enthusiasm in higher education. The challenge for educators is how to build on the successes of small-scale interventions and expand them to all students at key points in their academic careers. As we stated in the introduction, we make the case that it is not enough for students to act; they must also believe that they have the power to act in ways that result in their success:

> Although what students *do* is a key factor in their academic performance, it is increasingly clear that student success also depends greatly on what students *believe*, both about themselves as learners and about their learning environment. (p. 2)

It is not an overstatement to say that we believe the ideas shared in this book can make a significant difference in student success. This is especially true for those who historically have been least likely to succeed because of their own beliefs, reinforced over the years by a culture of exclusivity and a competitive, sink-or-swim environment.

If we return a final time to Richard's mindset story, we can see in him what we all might face if we employ the strategies and interventions discussed here. He sees the need to improve the success of the students he serves. He already tracks their progress for the grant program at his institution and has had some success: Students are retained and graduating at the benchmarks that were set. However, Richard knows he might be able to do much more for his underrepresented students. He wonders whether his work could connect with the institution's broader mission to improve overall retention and graduation rates—important outcomes for any institution, but certainly not the only measures of student success. Richard views his students through a lens of growth mindset, yet he knows not everyone at the institution feels the same about low-income, first-generation students. He also demonstrates resilience himself, through his ability to stay focused on his goals despite the challenges he faces in navigating a traditional college culture and institutional bureaucracy.

As educators, we frequently face situations that resemble Richard's. Knowing that others have faced similar challenges and have overcome them can help us stay the course during difficult times. In other words, the learning mindsets that help students make significant academic progress can also help educators in their efforts to design, implement, and improve student success initiatives.

Campus Conversations

The following questions are provided to begin conversations with key players on campus and as starting points for implementing change:

- What do the institution's data reveal about the current state of student achievement?

- What more do you want to know about student success at your institution?

- Who needs to be involved in the conversation about assessment? Who fills what roles in the assessment process?

- Who owns the data? What are the challenges to accessing, disseminating, and discussing it? What are the opportunities involved?

- How will you use data to create goals for the assessment process?

- What kinds of change do you hope to see from implementing a learning-mindset intervention?

Next Steps

The following steps are suggestions for moving from exploration to action:

1. Use Table 7.1 to begin to brainstorm your goals, outcomes, and methods for an intervention. Consider the multiple outcomes that could be part of your overall assessment plan.

2. Ask the following questions as part of the initial process for deciding what type of intervention to employ:

   - What are the goals we are trying to achieve?
   - What kind of intervention(s) is best suited to achieve those goals?
   - How do we know we are using the intervention correctly?
   - How will we know if the intervention worked?

3. After determining your intervention, discuss the following with your team:

   - What is the optimal timing of the intervention (e.g., pre-matriculation, first semester, second year, pre-graduation)?
   - What is the appropriate occasion for the intervention (e.g., summer registration, bridge program, first week of classes)?

4. Check out High Point University's Quality Enhancement Plan (QEP) on growth mindset at http://www.highpoint.edu/qep/. Jim Trammel, the institution's QEP director, has assembled a wealth of resources as well as a plan for implementing and assessing growth mindset.

Table 7.1
Sample Assessment Plan for Institutions

Institutional mission	Goals	Intended outcomes	Assessment methods
What aspect of the institutional mission does this address?	What do you hope to accomplish with the intervention?	What would student success look like?	What data will you collect?
	Goal 1:		
	Goal 2:		

References

Astin, A. W. (1991). *Assessment for excellence: The philosophy and practice of assessment and evaluation in higher education.* Washington, DC: American Council on Education/Oryx Press Series on Higher Education.

High Point University. (n.d.). *Quality Enhancement Plan.* Retrieved from Quality Enhancement Plan homepage, http://www.highpoint.edu/qep/

Strauss, V. (2017, April 21). The list of test-optional colleges and universities keeps growing—despite College Board's latest jab. *The Washington Post.* Retrieved from https://wapo.st/2CPwhUT

Appendix

A Glossary of Terms

21st century skills

Specific literacies, as outlined by the National Council of Teachers of English (NCTE), including the ability to "develop proficiency and fluency with the tools of technology; build intentional cross-cultural connections and relationships with others so to pose and solve problems collaboratively and strengthen independent thought; design and share information for global communities to meet a variety of purposes; manage, analyze, and synthesize multiple streams of simultaneous information; create, critique, analyze, and evaluate multimedia texts; [and] attend to the ethical responsibilities required by these complex environments" (http://www2.ncte.org/statement/21stcentdefinition; Introduction).

academic behaviors

Actions or practices that are commonly associated with being a good student, such as attending class, coming to class prepared, staying alert and engaged during class, participating in class activities and discussions, and devoting out-of-school time to studying and completing homework (Farrington et al., 2012; Introduction).

academic mindsets

An individual's attitudes or beliefs about themselves in relation to their academic work. Positive academic mindsets motivate students to engage in the positive academic behaviors associated with improved academic performance (Farrington et al., 2012; Chapter 1).

academic perseverance

A student's tendency to complete academic work satisfactorily and on time, despite challenges, distractions, or other obstacles in their personal or academic environment (Farrington et al., 2012; Chapter 1).

achievement gap

"When one group of students [such as students grouped by race/ethnicity, gender] outperforms another group and the difference in average scores for the two groups is statistically significant [that is, larger than the margin of error]" (NCES, 2018; Introduction).

affinity groups

Diverse subgroups within the community who often benefit from mutual support. These involve individuals who share salient identities and experiences (Chapter 1).

appreciative advising

An advising philosophy that focuses on advisor and student interactions around six phases: disarm, discover, dream, design, deliver, and don't settle (Bloom, Hutson, & He, 2008; Chapter 2).

belonging uncertainty

A phenomenon that occurs in academic settings for "members of socially stigmatized groups [who] are more uncertain of the quality of their social bonds and thus more sensitive to issues of social belonging" (Walton & Cohen, 2007, p. 82; Chapter 1).

character strengths

Those virtues or traits that lead to increased happiness and are considered good or positive by a vast majority of cultures, such as wisdom, courage, justice, gratitude, optimism, curiosity (Peterson & Seligman, 2004; Introduction).

classroom community

Comprising both a teacher and students, a learning environment where students feel safe and are encouraged by both teacher and peers to learn, express ideas, and teach one another. In such a community, students work toward a common goal and hold each other accountable for expectations in the classroom (Chapter 5).

classroom culture

The expectations, rewards, consequences, and even seating arrangements that encourage learning and limit distractions to the learning process. In creating this type of culture, teachers attempt to transform their classrooms from mere spaces for learning to environments where students feel safe and empowered to learn (Chapter 5).

crisis of confidence

When a student experiences extreme self-doubt about their abilities during a challenging homework assignment, a new section or module of content, a difficult test or assignment, or a cumulative course experience, such as a final exam (Yeager, 2017; Chapter 3).

educationally purposeful activities

Activities, involvement, or behaviors that are highly correlated with academic success and are characterized by student time-on-task, use of institutional resources, and meaningful student–faculty or student–peer interactions around substantive topics (Kuh, Kinzie, Schuh, & Whitt, 2005; Introduction).

everyday phrases

Statements reflecting growth mindset and the process of learning (Yeager, 2014). For example, "I see all of you working hard, and that's going to pay off. Your grade may not reflect that right now, but in a few weeks, you'll see how your hard work has laid the foundation for the rest of the semester." (Chapter 3).

fixed mindset

The belief that there is little one can do to influence their intelligence; that is, some people are born smart while others are not (Dweck, 2006; Chapter 1).

flourishing

A holistic view of well-being, encompassing engagement, meaning, positive emotions, rewarding relationships, and accomplishments (Seligman, 2012; Chapter 1).

formative assessment

Feedback that provides guidance for improvement; it is diagnostic rather than evaluative (Chapter 3).

grit

Passion and perseverance for long-term goals (Duckworth, 2016; Chapter 1).

growth mindset

The belief that one's intellectual abilities can grow through hard work, determination, and the correct strategies (Dweck, 2006; Chapter 1).

implicit bias

Unconscious, automatic responses rooted in assumptions about others. These are often based on race, ethnicity, or gender (Payne, Niemi, & Doris, 2018; Chapter 4).

intersectionality

Social vulnerabilities compounded by the intersection of class, race/ethnicity, gender, nationality, or sexuality as a result of discrimination (Chapter 1).

lay theory

The idea that challenges posed by the college transition are common and can get better; moreover, that any struggles during the transition are not proof of a lack of belonging or promise (Yeager et al., 2016); refers to the universal, human propensity for developing implicit models that help organize our understanding of the world (Chapter 1).

learning environment

The setting for teaching and learning, including the physical environment; cultural context; characteristics, attitudes, and behaviors of the teacher; and characteristics, attitudes, and behaviors of the students (Introduction).

learning mindsets

Key determinants in what students actually learn, they involve how students think about themselves as learners and about the learning environment (Dweck, Walton, & Cohen, 2014). Our view is that these mindsets have broad application across learning contexts, both in and outside of formal academic environments (Introduction).

mindset moments

Opportunities for employees to share how they have exhibited growth mindset or resilience or felt a sense of belonging, through the actions of students or another employee. These can occur with small groups (e.g., at the beginning of a meeting) and be shared with larger groups (Chapter 2).

noncognitive factors

A broad term referring to an expansive collection of skills, strategies, attitudes, and behaviors that positively influence academic performance but are not measured by traditional cognitive or standardized tests (Farrington et al., 2012; see also Heckman, 2008; Nagaoka et al., 2013; Sparkman, Maulding, & Roberts, 2012; Introduction).

opportunity gap

Refers to educational disadvantages experienced by low-income students compared to those from higher-income families, such as inadequate school funding, facilities, course offerings, and instruction (Chapter 4).

professional development plan

A record developed by an individual employee to highlight their professional goals as well as professional development opportunities that can help them achieve those goals. A plan can also state what the employee will learn by capitalizing on such opportunities and how this can help them achieve the stated goals (Chapter 6).

psychosocial interventions

Actions performed to bring about changes in people's behaviors, attitudes, or thinking (Introduction).

resilience

"The process of adapting well in the face of adversity … it involves bouncing back or steering through difficult experiences. Resilience is also an ongoing process that requires time and effort" (APA, 2011; Masten, 2014; Chapter 1).

self-authorship

The capacity to act on one's own purposes, values, feelings, and meanings, rather than those of external authorities (Chapter 2).

self-handicapping

A strategy to save face in the context of potential failure by not exerting effort or downplaying the importance of a performance (Jones & Berglas, 1978; Chapter 1).

sense of belonging

The belief that one is part of a group (Chapter 1).

social belonging

"A sense that one has positive relationships with others" (Walton & Cohen, 2007, p. 1147; Introduction).

social skills

Interpersonal abilities such as cooperation, assertion, responsibility, and empathy (Farrington et al., 2012; Introduction).

soft skills

A constellation of interpersonal skills such as communication, listening, conflict management, and time management (Introduction).

stereotype threat

Underperformance, intellectual or otherwise, because of concerns about fulfilling a negative stereotype pertinent to one's identity (Steele, 2010; Chapter 1).

student success

A holistic phenomenon that includes intellectual, emotional, social, ethical, physical, and spiritual development (Cook-Sather, 2018; Cuseo, 2007). It is the degree to which students experience learning, growth, improvement, and change (Dweck, 2006) across a variety of domains, both in and outside the classroom (Introduction).

summative assessment

Feedback given at the end of a period of instruction, generally evaluative in nature (Chapter 3).

unproductive mindsets/beliefs

Beliefs, attitudes, or values that, in contrast to productive learning mindsets, lead students to disengage from their educational experiences or engage in behaviors associated with academic failure (e.g., failing to attend class, ask for help, or complete academic work; Chapter 2).

wise criticism

A "combination of an explicit invocation of high standards and an appropriate assurance that the student in question could meet such standards" (Cohen, Steele, & Ross, 1999, p. 1310; Chapter 3).

Index

NOTE: Page numbers with italicized *f* or *t* indicate figures or tables respectively.

B

beliefs, internal. See also productive beliefs; unproductive beliefs or mindsets
  learning-mindset interventions and, 39, 42, 45–46
  resilience and, 25*t*
  social-belonging intervention and, 75
  student success and, 2–3
beliefs, shared. *See* mission statements
belonging. *See also* noncognitive factors; social belonging
  on campus, students' rating of, 122
  Campus Conversations on, 26
  college story and, vii
  developing feelings of, 8
  experiences reinforcing, xiv
  faculty and staff developing sense of, 107
  faculty incorporating tools of, 61
  faculty recruitment and, 92–93, 92*t*
  growth-mindset interventions and, 73–74
  growth of, through effort, 42
  Human Bingo promoting, 111–112
  intervention during summer orientation, 37
  interventions, assessment and, 121
  learning mindsets and, 13–15
  listing of friends and, viii
  mindset moments and, 44
  mission statement on, 89
  resilience, growth mindset and, 25
  sophomore transitions and, 43
  teaching faculty and staff to help students develop, 107
  training on promoting, 111
belonging uncertainty, 14
Black students. *See also* James's story; minority students; racial–ethnic–cultural

identity
  growth-mindset interventions for, 73–74
  listing of friends and, viii
  middle school, interventions with, 75
  mSuccess intervention and, 79–80
  predominantly White campus and, 13
  recruiting and retaining, 77
  social-belonging intervention and, viii–ix, 55, 74–75
bouncing back, resilience and, 23, 24
brain growth, learning process and, 54
brain teasers, role-specific development and, 112
brevity, mSuccess intervention and, 80
Brigham Young University (BYU), 36
Brooks, J. E., 19
Brown v. Board of Education, 66
Bunting, B. D., xii–xiv

C

campus collaboration, mSuccess and, 81
Campus Conversations
  on achievement gap and, 82–83
  on assessment, 125
  on campus culture, 102
  on faculty messaging, 61
  on first-year students and other transitions, 46
  on learning mindsets, xii, 7, 26–27
  on professional development, 115–116
campus culture
  Campus Conversations on, 102
  celebrating, 101
  Daniel's story, 87–88
  evidence of, 91–101
  faculty's role in, 62
  growth mindset of administrators and, 26

About the Authors

Amy Baldwin is the director of Student Transitions and a faculty member at the University of Central Arkansas. She wrote *The Community College Experience*, the first student success textbook for community college students, as well as *The First-Generation College Experience*, the first student success textbook for first-generation college students. Other texts she has written include *The College Experience* and *A High School Parent's Guide to College Success*. As a national expert on student success, Baldwin provides workshops for faculty and staff on topics such as teaching first-year and first-generation college students. Baldwin earned an EdD in higher education administration from the University of Arkansas at Little Rock and an MA in British Literature at Washington University in St. Louis.

Bryce Bunting is assistant clinical professor in the Counseling and Career Center at Brigham Young University. Bryce's varied work in higher education has spanned orientation and the first-year experience, peer education, common reads, summer bridge programs for student athletes, and early-alert initiatives. Recognized as a national expert in the first-year experience and peer education, Bryce regularly facilitates workshops and consults with faculty members, senior administrators, academic advisors, and higher education professionals on student success issues. Bryce currently serves as the editor of the *Journal of Peer Learning*. He holds a bachelor's degree in exercise science, an MS in instructional design, and a PhD in educational psychology.

Doug Daugherty is the executive dean at Indiana Wesleyan University and a licensed clinical psychologist. Prior to serving in administration, he was a professor of psychology and addictions counseling for many years. His interests include student belonging, formation, and success; positive psychology; faculty development, diversity and inclusion; and smartphone delivery of positive psychology interventions. Daugherty completed a PsyD in clinical psychology at Indiana State University and an MA in clinical psychology at Ball State University. He has served as program evaluator for several problem-solving courts and is the founder of a faith-based recovery home in Marion, Indiana.

Latoya Hardman Lewis is director of Academic Initiatives and Partnerships at Lone Star College-Tomball. In this role, she oversees all P-16 initiatives for the college, including dual credit and early college high school. She is also responsible for the college's grit and growth mindset initiatives. Latoya has worked as a high school English teacher as well as faculty for developmental English and education courses. Additionally, Latoya is a contributing author to *Complete the Agenda in Higher Education: Challenge Beliefs About Student Success.* She created the Instructional Technology Certification Program and teaches college instructors how to infuse technology effectively into any classroom setting. Latoya received her undergraduate degree from the University of Houston–Downtown, where she studied English literature. She received her MA from City College of New York and is working on her PhD in higher education leadership and policy studies at the University of Houston.

Tim Steenbergh is professor of psychology and chair of Behavioral Sciences at Indiana Wesleyan University and a licensed clinical psychologist. His interests in helping people flourish have led to various endeavors. However, over the past few years, his research has focused on student success and the use of mobile technology to promote student flourishing. Steenbergh completed his undergraduate studies in psychology, an MA in clinical psychology at Ball State University, a PhD in clinical psychology and behavioral medicine at the University of Memphis, and a postdoctoral fellowship in clinical health psychology and medical education at Michigan State University and Genesys Regional Medical Center.